MW00366487

She, He & Finding Me

An inspiring true story about
female-to-male gender reassignment

TJ BARGANSKI

She, He & Finding Me– 1st ed.
An inspiring true story about female-to-male gender reassignment
TJ Barganski
Cover Design by AlyBlue Media, LLC
Interior Design by AlyBlue Media LLC
Published by AlyBlue Media, LLC

ISBN: 978-1-950712-35-9
AlyBlue Media, LLC
Ferndale, WA 98248
www.AlyBlueMedia.com

PRINTED IN THE UNITED STATES OF AMERICA

Dedication

This book is dedicated with love to the friends
and family who supported me, then and now.

She, He & Finding Me

Contents

She, He & Finding Me

BY THERESA WATERS, ARNP

I highly recommend reading this inspirational story of TJ Barganski's transformation from female to male. I've been in awe of his resilience and courage in the ten years I have known him. As a therapist, I'm confident this book can help anyone who is personally grappling with feelings about their sexual identity. It can also be a resource for those in the helping profession or for loved ones to gain insight and empathy in order to better understand these complex challenges.

TJ's style of describing his experiences is heart-wrenching yet tempered with a dose of humor that will make it impossible to put his book down until you devour it from cover to cover.

THERESA WATERS, ARNP, PLLC

BY TJ BARGANSKI

Preface

The story you're about to read is the honest, candid truth about the events of my life before, during, and after transitioning from a she to a he, and ultimately to me.

People find my life story interesting because they see it as an adventure. Raised in a Mormon family and feeling like a boy attracted to girls is more like a living hell. My past is filled with drama, chaos, molestation, gender confusion, mental and physical abuse, learning difficulties, torment, and ridicule.

Aside from my Mormon family, growing up in the 1970s wasn't the best era to be candid about my truth. Yet, my body's gender contradicted my heart and soul. What could be worse than that? And yet, that's exactly my truth. From the moment I was born, my heart and soul felt like a boy. A boy who was attracted to girls.

And that's where this story begins.

She, He & Finding Me

CHAPTER ONE

My mother, my father

In 1963, my mom was living in Yuma, Arizona. I wouldn't think she had much to do in a town with triple-digit heat and tumbleweeds. When she told me stories, I imagined something like black and white episodes of *Twilight Zone*—people sipping sweet tea on their porch with fans trying to stay cool.

Mother—as she wanted to be called—was just nineteen years-old, living on her own in a trailer, working as a waitress in a local café. A tall, slim redhead, she had big green eyes and wore her hair in a tight beehive.

Mother occasionally went out with friends to a dance club called Honky-Tonk Inn, where all the local cowboys hung out. I envisioned something out of a John Wayne movie.

Mother said there were all kinds of tall, handsome cowboys dressed in boots, fancy collared shirts, and leather vests. She said some wore their jeans so tight that it hurt to look at 'em. That's where it all began.

One night at the Honky-Tonk, Mother met my biological father. Describing him as a tall, handsome blue-eyed Texan cowboy who had nothing in the personality department, Mother said he was so darn pretty, though. And those blue eyes, well, there was just something about him.

TJ's mother and father.

"Yes, he was quite the ladies' man," Mother would say, blinking her eyes. "But he was so, so beautiful."

Dad said they met when she backed into him and stepped on his boot. "Um, lady, you stepped on my boot!"

As she turned to reply, all she could do was stare and say, "You want to dance?"

They danced all night, apparently until at least August 1965. The dates are unclear when my parents actually married and then divorced. I've heard so many stories about their crazy meetings. Who knows what to believe? It's like the saying goes, there are three sides to every story. This is my version.

My parents got married and settled down. They lived in a rundown single-wide trailer next door to my grandparents, who were divorced but still lived together. They owned a large chunk of property that afforded them to have all their children and families live nearby. My three aunts and my parents all lived within walking distance of my paternal grandparents.

From what I know, my father was lazy by trade. On occasion when he needed money, he drove a semitruck to make a few dollars. Otherwise, his normal work ethic was doing nothing when he could.

In July 1964, Mother discovered she was pregnant. Both she and my father were only twenty-one, and although happy at the time, they were poor. Mother started to wonder about life with my father, and whether this was what she wanted for herself. Knowing she had married my father for his looks was not the best decision she ever made, but being pregnant wasn't the best time to leave.

Mother began to plan for a better future for herself and her unborn child. Her family had already moved from Arizona to California, and she planned to leave my father to join them when the time was right.

In March 1965, Mother delivered her firstborn, my sister Kari, and began planning her exit. The only thing she owned was a 1952 Chevy and the few dollars in her pocket. How was she going to get to her family in California?

April came and went, so did May, June, and July. Mother lived those months as if nothing was amiss. By mid-August, she was ready to make her move.

My father often wouldn't let Mother drive her own car to work, so she walked. On one of the hottest days on record, she was walking home when from across the field she could see my father and his dad doing something to her car. They had it up on blocks and although Mother couldn't quite make out what they were doing, she knew they were up to no good.

Mother started to run. As she got closer, she saw that they had switched out the brand new tires she had just bought for her old, bald tires. Madder than a hornet, she sprinted across the field, hurdled a barbwire fence, and out of breath yelled, "What the fuck do you think you're doing?"

Both my father and his father stood there. They had just sold her new tires for twenty dollars.

"Y'all better give me half that money!"

They only had a twenty-dollar bill, which proved to be to Mother's advantage. The time was right to leave.

Mother said, "I'll go to the store and get change, and bring you back ten."

She took the twenty-dollar bill, got into her car and drove straight to the trailer, packed what she could, picked up my sister Kari, went to the gas station to fill up the tank, and drove west to California. I've often wondered how long it took my father to figure out she wasn't coming back with the change.

Mother managed to make it to just outside San Diego when she ran out of both fuel and money. She called a relative who brought just enough gas for Mother to get to her final destination. Her plan was to stay with family until she could get on her feet. She would start a new life for her and her six-month-old daughter in California.

Mother found a waitressing job in San Diego and started to settle in, but then began to feel sick. At first, she thought it was stress or maybe the change in climate. Perhaps it was from working too much. She hadn't been seeing anyone and had been on birth control since my sister was born, so there was little chance of a pregnancy.

Perhaps she had a bladder infection and should go see the doctor. She made an appointment. The doctor examined her, left the room for a few minutes and then returned with a big smile. "Congratulations, Mrs. Barganski! You're pregnant!"

Stunned, my mother sat in silence until the words slipped quietly from her lips. "Thank you, I think."

How did this happen?

She didn't want another baby so soon, especially from my father. Further, she had a heart murmur and was told that another pregnancy could kill her. By now, it was too late. Mother couldn't send me back. She was in it for the long haul.

She prayed for a girl, not a boy.

*

CHAPTER TWO

Early family life

On May 3, 1966, Mother was out enjoying a few drinks and eating shrimp when I gave her the signal. She headed to the hospital in Point Loma, California, at about 9 p.m. The doctor himself was out having a few drinks and wasn't far away. The nurse prepared Mother for delivery, but the doctor still hadn't arrived. Time was passing and I was getting closer to making my entrance. Mother was in the middle of vomiting her shrimp dinner when the doctor finally stumbled into the delivery room. "Well, what, uh, we got here?" he slurred.

He caught me just in the nick of time and gave me a smack on the back. I was pink and all was well. The nurse was instructed to clean up my mom, and the doctor called it a night. It was 10:58 p.m.

Mother was taken to her room to rest and I was carted off to the nursery with all the other pinks and blues. But she could not rest, thanks to the sound of a wailing infant. She fought the urge to run down the hall and choke the life from it, or return it to where it came from. The crying suddenly got louder, and she wanted to scream, "Shut that kid up!"

Suddenly, she heard angry footsteps and then her door flew open. An irritated nurse came in and said in a loud aggravated voice, "Here! This is yours!"

Mother said the nurse practically threw me at her, and she had to catch me. The nurse spun around on her heels and left the room. When she did, my crying stopped.

Mother said I had the bluest eyes she had ever seen, and my hair was so white that it looked like I had none.

Not knowing whether I was going to be a boy or girl, she hadn't yet picked out a name. What was she going to call me? She couldn't leave until my birth certificate had a name.

My name has since led to lots of confusion. Some say my maternal grandmother named me, some say my mom named me. I was named after my mom, Terry, but went by TJ most of my life. Mother spelled it T-e-j-a-i, which caused me a lot of grief growing up, so now I just use the initials. Junior, not Jr., is my middle name. Lots of people ask about that, too.

I was less than a year old when Mother met a man from Malaysia. His name was Pete, and I suppose they dated for some time though Mother never shared too much detail about that time. I've heard bits and pieces from different people. One version was that my mother and grandmother had an argument after Mother married Pete, and off to Malaysia we went.

Mother planned to raise my sister Kari and I in Malaysia, and we lived there for at least a year. Mother said I was well liked because of my curly blonde hair, big blue eyes, and chubby goodness. Locals called me Gobs because my cheeks were so chunky.

TJ, age 2.

Much like her first marriage, the marriage to Pete was also short lived, partly due to the Vietnam war. It was 1967, and Malaysia was not that far away. Giant pythons roamed into our yard, and headless bodies bound in barbwire began to wash up on beaches.

Many horrible things were now happening and Mother didn't want us exposed to it all. Although she loved Pete and enjoyed living in Malaysia, she felt it had become unsafe and didn't want to risk the lives of her children.

We returned home to the U.S. when I was about two. Pete stayed behind. We ran into him years later. He told me he never forgot us, that he loved us very much, and always wondered what happened to us. Everyone has their own version of the story, and even though that chapter is closed, I will always be thankful for Pete's loving words.

Back in the states, Mother resumed life as a single woman with two young daughters. She got a job in the same restaurant in Point Loma where my aunt and grandmother waitressed. It was late 1968, and this was a decent way for a single mother to make a living and support her family.

For two years, Mother stayed single, worked, and raised us two girls. I suppose it was hard for her, as from an early age people thought I was a boy. I wanted to dress like a boy and was always getting into things.

One time I put her contact lens in my eyes, and then woke her up and said I had something in my eyes. She said, "No, TJ," and went back to sleep. I persisted to pester her, insisting I had something in my eyes. After the fourth attempt, she sat up. Her contacts were tinted green, and I had put them in my eyes. The correct eyes, too. The fun had just begun. By age two, I learned to whistle, talk like Donald Duck, get up and down high places, and cut my hair. Mother always said I was different, special.

I was four when Mother met a new man. His name was Glen and he worked as a dishwasher in the same restaurant. He was about nine years her junior. They dated a couple years, and he seemed to like Kari and I, and we grew up knowing no different. When Mother and Glen married, we thought he was our dad. We were now a normal Mormon family living in a cool house in Mira Mesa.

Glen is the man I would grow to love and call Dad. At my young age, I didn't think anything about this, really. Kari and I just accepted him into our lives as Dad. We were even in their wedding. I had to be a flower girl and throw flower petals from a basket as I walked down the aisle. I wanted to vomit. Oh, how I hated that dress! It was long and purple, and the top was made of lacy material. Mother even put a purple bow in my hair. I remember someone taking pictures of Kari and I wearing those stupid dresses. It was agony. How could anyone understand how it felt for me to wear a dress when I couldn't understand it myself? All I knew was that it felt totally awkward, unnatural, and I thought everyone was staring at me.

Any time I was forced to wear girly clothes, I felt an inner rage as though I was going to explode. Many times I did just that—I had violent outbursts no one could explain. I knew I would be beaten for acting out, yet despite knowing the consequences, I continued the same behavior.

I was five, Kari was six, and Mother was twenty-seven and getting married to Glen, her third husband who was just nineteen. What in the world could she have been thinking? She had just up and left her second husband and moved back from Malaysia without so much as a divorce. She meets this young guy at their mutual place of employment, ropes him in and marries him.

Kari and I went by Glen's surname. We didn't know our own was legally different until my mother and Glen divorced. I now go by my legal surname, my birthfather's last name.

Mother and Glen went to Catalina Island for their honeymoon. Kari and I stayed with our new grandparents. We also had a new aunt and uncle. We seemed to be there a lot, and grew to love them as family.

I believe children who feel unloved will reach out to anyone who might give them affection. I was a fat kid who wet the bed, and my new grandmother snapped me with rubber bands to punish me for it. They called me Pee-pee Pants.

They often said, "You're so pretty! Why do you want to look like a little boy?"

I wish I could have found a way to say, "Because I want to be one, that's why."

I'm sure that if I had been able to speak up, rubber bands would have been the least of my worries. Yet in spite of it all, I loved Glen's family. They were the only family I knew.

Mother and Glen stayed married for about eight years, during which time my younger sister Sara was born on my eighth birthday. I had no clue that the man I'd come to know as Dad was not my father. I didn't discover the truth until after they divorced.

I grew up in southern California, where the proximity to Disneyland and Hollywood made it one of the best places to live as a kid.

From left: Mother, TJ (front), Kari (back), and Glen holding Sarah.

I came from the classic Mormon family. We lived in what was then an upper-class neighborhood. My childhood was a lot like *Leave It to Beaver*, with a dose of abuse thrown in at the hands of Mother. I also felt like a freak, an outcast, a nobody. I was the ultimate definition of a real loner, though at that young age, couldn't yet understand why.

Mother enrolled me in school, spelling my name Tejai. It caused many problems throughout childhood and most of my adolescent years. People couldn't pronounce it. Teachers tried to call my name, look around the room, and then back at their attendance sheet until finally they would call, "Tea? Tia, um, Teehe . . . umm, oh umm . . ."

I often rescued them from their misery by quietly saying, "It's TJ."

"What is it, again?"

"TJ," I'd repeat with a sigh.

"One more time, please?"

"TJ!"

I would shout it out, which immediately resulted in class laughter and snickers. Children whispered among themselves, "Is that a girl or a boy?"

Wanting to disappear, I sank down in my chair as far as I could. The teachers did nothing to stop the kids from laughing at me.

Why did they not know I was a girl? My mother sent me to school in pigtails. How many boys went to school in red ditto pants, ruffled shirt, Wallabee shoes, and pigtails with big colored bobbles adorning the rubber bands? My first-grade teacher tagged the whole name debacle with the statement, "Oh! I was looking for a little boy, honey. I'm sorry."

She didn't know how prophetic that would be.

To this day, people continue to ask about my name and what the initials stand for. For a long time, I hated my name and didn't like to tell them. I didn't even spell it the way my mother did, T-e-j-a-i. With today's exotic names, nobody would probably question it. Yet people remain curious about what TJ stands for. When I tell them, more often than not I hear something along the lines of, "Wow! Is your middle name really Junior? Then who's Terry Senior?"

When I tell them it's my mother, the reaction is, "No way! Wow. You're really named after your mom?"

I used to get mad when people teased me about my name until I learned to make a joke of it. I would retort, "Yes, that's what Polacks do, I guess. One of my sisters was named after my dad and I was named after my mother. You know how Polacks do everything backwards?"

I'm also half Native American, and often added, "I'm half Polack and half Indian. So don't stand behind me because my arrow goes backwards."

People just laughed and soon forgot about my name altogether. I'm okay with my name now. It served me well in later years because I didn't have to change my name when I had my gender changed on my birth certificate.

In 1973, my parents drove a brown Pinto and we lived on Jade Coast Drive in Mira Mesa, California. As a first-grader, I had a bright purple bike with a banana seat and a flower basket on the front. How I hated that thing! What were my parents thinking? I wanted nothing more than to destroy every plastic petal adorning that stupid white basket. I felt like those flowers were visible for miles, embarrassing me even before people could make out who was riding the bright purple bike.

One day I just ripped the basket clean off the bike. From then on, I happily rode that bike all over. In those days, we were able to go places alone, like to the park, without our parents having to worry. We just had to be back by dark.

I spent most of my time playing with a bunch of boys in the nearby field. I didn't play with many of the neighborhood girls because they taunted me, telling me I was a boy. After all, I looked like a boy and had a boy's name. Further, I had nothing in common with girls. I didn't play house or with dolls. I didn't dress up or put on makeup. I didn't wish for an Easy Bake oven. I wanted a gun, a guitar, a minibike, and a G.I. Joe.

The boys and I often threw dirt clods at girls riding by on their bikes. I especially took pleasure throwing dirt clods at the girls who tormented me. A well-aimed clod hitting its target was very satisfying. The girls would run home crying as the boys and I laughed.

One time, I was riding my bike as fast as I could to get away from some kids who were chasing me. Thinking I was a boy, they wanted to beat me up.

"Hey, little boy!"

"Hey kid, stop!"

I looked back to see how close they were, and slammed into the side of a camper, smashing my ear. I had never felt such pain. My ear was red hot and my bike was bent. I went home and told my mother what happened. She paid no attention to the incident at all. "Well, if you dressed like a little girl, they wouldn't say those things to you."

I had zero support.

I didn't understand when people said to act like a girl, and dress like a girl. It enraged me and I acted out by screaming and punching walls. Back then such behavior was labeled as hyperactivity. At about this same time, I also started wetting the bed, which really made my parents mad. No one knew what to do. Mother decided to seek medical treatment, and took me to several different doctors. One after the other didn't seem to know what was wrong with me.

One time, I was hooked up to a machine that had all kinds of colored wires with small pins at the end that were attached to various spots on my head. I was made to lie down for what felt like hours, and had no clue what was taking place. It wasn't until I was much older when I found out my mother had me tested for mental deficiency. It was a brainwave test, and she was told I had a scar on the lower left side of my brain that gathered static energy. She was told that when there was no room for more energy, it would explode, therefore causing me to have outbursts.

The doctor told my mother this behavior was normal in little boys my age. He said I would soon outgrow it, but in the meantime he offered a prescription for Ritalin.

My mother wasn't sure she heard him correctly, so she said, "You know this is my daughter Tejai, right?"

The doctor seemed a bit puzzled as he looked at my mother and said, "Oh, I'm so sorry. No, I didn't. I, I...well, you do only see this condition in young boys so I just thought he, I mean she, was a boy."

Mother filled the prescription and started giving it to me in hopes it would help. Instead, it turned me into a zombie. I had a hard time staying alert and began sleeping in class.

I was kept on the Ritalin for a while and then Mother took me off cold turkey. Instead of taking me back to the doctor to get the dose adjusted, Mother took it upon herself to just discontinue the prescription. In the long run, that decision was a disservice to me and my education.

My gender confusion continued to grow with afterschool activities and societal girl clubs. Mother was a Bluebird troop leader, so naturally my sister and I became Bluebirds. My sister loved it. I hated it. Why did I have to wear the stupid uniform and sit around with a bunch of girls I didn't like, who didn't like me either? Why did my mother continually want me to participate in these girl rituals when it obviously made my life a living hell?

In looking back, I believe now that my mother was hoping against hope that I would show some sign of actually acting like a girl. But I absolutely hated the red ribbon in my hair, the blue skirt, all of it. I hated the whole getup. I screamed every time she put a dress near me. As a compromise and most likely to keep the peace, Mother often allowed me to wear shorts under my dress.

On some level, I do think my mother did want to love me but just couldn't allow herself to, for some reason. That's the way it felt. I was an odd child with some sort of underlying problem Mother couldn't figure out. Therefore, I was an easy target upon whom to vent her anger and frustration.

Mother had a deep hatred for my father, and every time she looked at me, she saw him, which made her dislike me even more. But because I was her child, I believe she tried desperately in her own way to love me but having psychological problems of her own only escalated her behavior toward me.

Mother also had a tendency toward Parent Alienation Syndrome. She kept us away from family members at times. Years later I discovered that Mother had dated her step-father, my step-grandfather, throughout her marriages, as well as her husband's brothers and father. Looking back on all this now, I believe she suffered from a Cinderella complex, always looking for her Prince Charming, using sex and looks to manipulate men into giving her what she wanted. She wanted to have a fairytale life but in the end was stuck with nothing but her kids each time, and it was us who paid the price. In some ways, perhaps she was searching for something within, just as I was. She's still searching to this day.

My mother said she always knew there was something different about me, she just didn't know what. She had no idea what gay, transgender, transvestite, or any of those things were, let alone what they meant. If she had to do it all over again, she claims she would have just saved me years of torture and raised me as a boy. I am not sure that's true, because I am not sure if my mother ever really loved me.

I continued to feel like an outcast and a misfit at school. Children threw sand in my face and pushed me down on the playground. One time, I refused to come to the reading circle and instead ran to the back of the room. The teacher jerked me up by my arm and said she'd had enough of my behavior, and that I'd have to stay outside where the bad children go.

"You can come back in when you've learned to be good!"

I was also sent outside for not wanting to sit down in class. I had so much rage, an unexplainable inner fury. It felt overwhelming and I didn't know where it was coming from.

One day, the anger boiled over and I punched a school window, breaking it. With a deep laceration on my wrist and blood everywhere, I was rushed to the nurse's office and my mother was called.

Afterward, I was stone-faced and registered no emotion. I paid no attention to anyone.

Mother exclaimed, "What's wrong with you? Are you crazy?"

I received a multitude of stitches that left a scar as a reminder of that painful day.

I returned to school a few days later. Mother dressed me in a white long-sleeved shirt. I think she was actually trying to help by concealing the white bandage wrapped around my right wrist. She walked me into class and I saw the window had been boarded up. I kept my hand behind my back so no one could see it. Everyone was staring at me. They were all sitting up front in that reading circle. I don't know who was more scared, me or the teacher. She nervously invited me to sit with the rest of the kids.

"Whenever you're ready, you can come join us," she said very kindly.

For the rest of the year I was line leader, and not one kid made fun of me in those remaining months. But that didn't help the fact that I continued to feel like an outcast and was now starting to have twinges of depression. After all, I was still a stupid girl—nothing changed that miserable fact.

The stay in Mira Mesa came to an end when Mother and Dad bought a home in an upper-class neighborhood in San Carlos, in San Diego county. We moved into an average sized three-bedroom, two-bath home with a living room, kitchen, and a garage.

The backyard was a feature I came to appreciate because it led to the city drainage area, a place where I could escape. I also had my own room where I could hide in the darkness of my closet. It was my sanctuary where I pretended to be someone else. It was so dark in that closest that I couldn't even see my hand, so I knew no one could see me for what I was—a lousy girl.

I often wished I were dead. At night I would lay down in the bathtub and allow the water to cover me while keeping my eyes open. I felt a strange calmness under the water and wished I could drown.

Why was I born a girl? I had to learn early on how to be emotionless and uncaring to survive the inner turmoil.

Some children start identifying with the opposite gender as early as toddlerhood

CENTER FOR GENDER AFFIRMING MEDICINE
AKRON CHILDREN'S HOSPITAL (2019)

CHAPTER THREE

Growing pains

In second grade, I went to a new school called Forward Elementary, which meant new teachers and new kids. Once again, I felt put on display. The teacher called out my name incorrectly several times. All the kids snickered, wondering whether I was a boy or girl.

My anger grew but there was no window to punch, so I threw a chair at the teacher. I was immediately marched to the principal's office, and my mother was called yet again. I knew I was going to get a beating when I got home. I didn't care.

What else could anyone possibly do to me that would make my life any worse? It would have been so much easier if I had been born a boy. These things would not be happening to me if that had been the case. Why wasn't I born a boy? I desperately hated being a girl. I despised girl clothes, girl toys, any thing and everything about being a girl. As far as I was concerned, life sucked.

Sure enough, when I got home, I got a beating and was sent to my room. I retreated to the safety of my dark closet for as long as possible. When Dad got home, I knew I was going to get hit with a belt or something worse.

I'm sure my parents' frustration was growing alongside my own. In looking back, I guess I can say then that I identified as a boy, yet at age eight, I was too young to articulate it.

I returned to school and was placed in another class, one reserved for special education students. When I opened the door, I saw three boys sitting in the classroom. I would make four. Just think, the four of us would be together throughout our elementary years in the same class!

When I walked in, the teacher was sitting at her desk. A small woman, she was dressed in a green wool pantsuit with a yellow ruffled shirt. She gave me a big smile, came over, put her arm around me and in a kind voice said, "I am Ms. Farley. This is where you can sit."

I had a desk at the front of the class. Ms. Farley was my teacher for the next two years, and was one of the nicest I had.

Her breath always smelled of coffee but she never said an unkind word. Further, nobody in class ever questioned me about who or what I was.

I was the token student. In fact, I became teacher's pet. I could feel that Ms. Farley accepted me, and so did those boys.

Us four boys hung around together both during school and after. It was always Ricky, Rod, Buddy and me. They often argued over who would get to sit by me during lunch. I never thought of them like that, of course. I just thought of them as my second-grade buddies. On occasion, they tried to give me a kiss or hold my hand. I wondered what the hell they were doing. When they acted like that, I thought my friends had somehow transformed into weird little creeps. I didn't want to hold their sweaty little hands or kiss them. Gross! I would sock 'em, and then they would stop it.

By age nine, I knew I was attracted to girls. As Mormons, we often attended church gatherings and I had a bad crush on one lady there. She was the only reason I looked forward to going to church. I watched for her every Sunday. She looked just like the actress Lynda Carter who played Wonder Woman on TV. She had the most beautiful face, stunning grayish-blue eyes, and lovely tan skin. I thought about her all the time and every so often she would catch me staring at her. She would wink and I would smile with embarrassment and sink down in to my dad's arm. He'd mumble, "What are you doing? Sit up!"

After a while, she quit coming to our church and I never saw her again.

When I was nine years-old, I became very ill with a high fever and something that resembled a rash all over my body. My nose began to bleed and wouldn't stop.

Mother took me to the hospital where I was diag-

TJ (age 9).

nosed with idiopathic thrombocytopenic purpura, a bleeding disorder that causes the body's immune system to attack and destroy healthy platelets, and prevents blood from clotting normally. Blood wept from the pores of my skin; even my urine was bloody. All over my body were broken blood vessels that had to be cleaned daily. I remember undergoing a spinal tap, which was very painful.

The church elders came to my hospital room, laid their hands on my head, and prayed over me. Other family members had to visit through a window. My classmates sent cards that were hung in my hospital room.

A little boy in the next room was diagnosed with the same illness and died. I remember thinking why should they care if I die? They hate me anyway. The strange thing was, I didn't care, either. But survive I did, and once I regained my health and was back to normal, so was family life.

I continued to feel different, wet my bed and had an inner rage. By now it was abundantly clear that something about me was different. I was an oddball who was never quite accepted.

Outside Ricky, Rod and Buddy, most of my playmates came from church where girls from primary group, which was like Sunday school except it was held on Wednesday nights, were separated from the boys. It was supposed to teach reverence and the role of the female's place in the home.

We attended church every Sunday and Wednesday night, sometimes more. I had to wear a dress every time. That was the one constant in my young life—it always felt unnatural to put on a dress, let alone fancy shoes and stockings. Beside the sheer misery of it all, it felt as though everyone was looking at me as if something was wrong. I was never quite accepted.

I did have one friend, Stephanie, who didn't care what other kids thought. Rail-thin with large blonde ringlets, she had big eyes that were a pretty shade of blue. Her mother often had her in dance class such as tap or jazz, or some other entertainment outlet. Although she was just my friend, I had a crush on her. At our young age, she and I planned to buy a sports car, serve on our mission together, and attend Brigham Young University. I suppose I would have done just about anything to be with her.

Stephanie lived up the road from our house. My younger sister and her younger brother were going to marry in the temple, so we expected to become family. The last time I saw her was when Mother made me perform in the church spring sing. Mother curled my hair so it bounced like coils. I wore white buckle shoes with lace socks, and a ridiculous pastel flowered dress all the girls in primary class had to wear when we performed onstage. I wanted to die.

The routine consisted of singing, dancing, and twirling umbrellas to a song. It felt as though the audience was watching a little boy in a dress doing a wretched dance routine. It was beyond humiliating, and I started to cry.

I felt uncomfortable anytime I was forced to wear a dress or one-piece swimsuit. The swimsuit was especially traumatic. As I got older, it was apparent I would need to wear a swimsuit at the beach or pool. As conservative Mormons, our faith prohibited girls from wearing anything else.

During puberty, I had become a bit chubby. I wanted to wear shorts and a T-shirt, but my mother always said no. She insisted I wear a one-piece swimsuit and, of course, I hated it. I wore shorts over it and refused to take my shirt off. Besides, I didn't go in the water anyway. I had developed a dreadful fear of the water.

I used to swim with my dad in Mission Bay. There is a small island in the middle, and he and I would swim out to the island and back. That all changed when the movie *Jaws* came out. It was released when I was nine years-old, and my parents took us to the drive-in theater to see it. I was terrified and tried to hide under the blankets and plug my ears. Did they understand my fear? No.

"We paid for this movie so you're going to watch it. It's not scary."

I had nightmares for years. I couldn't go into a swimming pool by myself, and often dreamed of sharks circling my bed at night, trapping me. I'd find myself stuck in dreams I couldn't get out of. Soon I had to sleep with the lights on.

0.7% of teens age 13 to 17
identify as transgender

CENTER FOR GENDER AFFIRMING MEDICINE
AKRON CHILDREN'S HOSPITAL (2019)

CHAPTER FOUR

New school, same problems

By fourth grade, my parents' frustration, along with my own, was growing steadily. Because the elementary school accommodated special education students only through the third grade, I had to go to a new school across town. It was decided that I would ride my bike to and from. I was with the same kids from my third-grade class, along with a few new ones. Once again, I was the only girl.

My fourth-grade teacher, Mr. Rodarte, had a smile from ear-to-ear all the time. He was Hispanic and his hair looked just like Desi Arnaz from *I Love Lucy*. He wore his pants just like that too, along with dress shoes and a buttoned shirt. He always wore a tie with a handkerchief in his pocket.

Mr. Rodarte always kept a jar of Red Hot candies on his desk. When we got a good grade on a paper, he removed the candies with tweezers and gave them to us as a reward. He brought oranges from his tree at home and sliced them for an afternoon snack using the small pocketknife he always carried. He played with us at recess, and every once in a while gave us a knock on the head and said, "That's just because."

I spent fourth, fifth, and sixth grade with him, and he was good to me over those years. I was the only girl in a class of boys, yet I fit right in and didn't feel alone.

I did start to have some problems with other kids, though, some of whom were in my class. Being teacher's pet helped. Mr. Rodarte took me under his wing and never let anyone bother me, as though he knew I was different. I was exceptionally good at reading and had neat penmanship. I also told the best stories and seldom had trouble in class, just outside.

TJ's 6th grade photo

Everyone in school knew we were the special ed class, so kids called us retards, the stupid kids, dummies, and lots of other choice names. In those days, flipping someone off was the worst thing you could do, and one older boy did just that every chance he got unless Mr. Rodarte was around.

One day at recess, we were alone playing kickball when the kid came at us. He wore cuffed blue jeans and a white shirt. His dirty-blonde hair was parted off to the side yet waved down into his face. With fists balled up, he shouted, "Look at the retards trying to play ball! Where's your babysitter? Who's going to protect you now?"

We all stood there frozen like statues. Most boys didn't dare pick a fight with this ornery kid. When he approached me, I thought, *oh, why me, God?*

"Are you a boy? Are you?" he sneered.

I didn't answer, so he pressed on, "What? Are you stupid?"

My rage began to build as he continued taunting me. And then I snapped. It was as if something had taken over and I couldn't control myself. I began punching him and slammed his head into the sandy ground as kids around us screamed.

Suddenly, Mr. Rodarte and another teacher pulled us apart and yanked us to our feet. The bully, bloodied and crying, went with one teacher and I went with Mr. Rodarte to our class. With his usual ear-to-ear smile, Mr. Rodarte gave me a hug. "You sure let him have it! A good one right in the nose! But you know I have to take you to the office, right? Let's go."

And off we went, though I knew Mr. Rodarte was proud of me for sticking up for myself. That bully never bothered anyone in our class again. He may have never known whether a boy or girl beat him up that day, but was smart enough to steer clear of us from that day forward.

I truly think Mr. Rodarte loved each of us kids. He did his best to follow us as we grew into adults to make sure we made something of our lives.

After my sex change, he and his wife contacted me and we met in the Sears parking lot in El Cajon. He flashed his big crazy smile just as he did when I was in fourth grade, and said, "You were the prettiest little girl I ever did see. I still have all your little pictures. And now I see you have grown up to be a very handsome young man. I am very proud of you."

For a brief moment, he held me the same way he did when I was young. While talking, he cleared his throat and wiped his nose and eyes with that ever-present handkerchief.

After he composed himself, he said "Look! Even at my age I can still touch my toes. Do you remember me doing that every morning?"

He then demonstrated as though I didn't believe him.

I replied, "Yes, of course I remember! I never forgot you, not ever. How could I?"

Mr. Rodarte went on to tell me about the kids I went to school with, and some of the tragedies they suffered, which saddened him. We talked for a while and then I watched as he and his wife drove away.

Mr. Rodarte passed away on April 30, 2004. Because he was a World War II veteran, he was buried at Fort Rosecrans National Cemetery in Point Loma, California.

I will always remember him and his kindness.

41% of transgender individuals
are suicidal in their lifetime

AKRON CHILDREN'S HOSPITAL (2019)

CHAPTER FIVE

Who's your daddy?

The next year, Glen, whom I considered my dad, left the family and all hell broke loose. I was ten years-old. My rage continued to grow along with my sexual identity confusion. Mother was never around, and my two-year-old sister Sara demanded all her attention when she was.

My older sister Kari was eleven when she began experimenting with drugs and sex. Mother escalated our beatings. One day she beat Kari with wire hangers for going to school wearing a Danskin skirt.

One morning, Mother decided I hadn't done the dishes to her standard the night before. As I was leaving for school, she hit me on the head with a wooden clog. Admiring her handiwork, she said, "Here, put this ice on it so it will stop bleeding."

Mr. Rodarte knew something was wrong that morning. He came by and knocked me on the head in good fun, as he often did. When I flinched, he saw my head. He held me close, probably because it was all he could think of to help me feel better.

Child abuse was never really addressed in those days; you simply didn't say anything to anyone. People just kept hush-hush about certain things, including that. Maybe Mr. Rodarte said nothing for fear something worse might happen to me if he had. I never asked why this incident was swept under the rug. I have a scar from that wooden clog, and when I get asked about it, I tell the truth. What else should I say?

At about that same time, my sister Kari and her friend started calling me a lezbo. Others called me a dyke. I know I rebelled against anything that had to do with being a girl, yet, at age ten, I had no clue what those names even meant.

One day when Glen came to pick up our younger sister Sara, Kari and I also wanted to go. My mother said, "No! He isn't your dad, and from now on you can go by your real last name as well."

Kari and I looked at each other in puzzlement. What was she talking about?

"What do you mean?" we asked.

Mother replied, "Your last name is Barganski, and you better learn to spell it, starting now."

We were devastated.

This latest bombshell fueled my anger. I walked to school trying to spell what was now my new last name. Mother then dropped a second bombshell. She was taking us to meet our real father that summer, a man we didn't know and who didn't know us. What were we supposed to call him? Dad?

As promised, that summer Mother took us to Arizona to meet our biological father. Our younger sister Sara stayed with the man who, up until that time, we believed was our dad.

I wondered what our real dad would be like. What did he look like? What would he think of me?

My aunt joined us for the trip. When we arrived at my paternal grandparents' large property, I saw a house on one side and a single-wide trailer on the other.

TJ (far left) with his sisters.

Mother told us to get out of the car. We approached the house and Mother knocked on the front door. A thin woman wearing a black beehive hairdo and holding a cigarette in one hand answered the door.

Mother said, "Does Ed live here? I'm Terry Lee."

The thin woman turned her head and screamed at the top of her lungs, "Ed!"

She waited a moment and then quietly mumbled, "Jesus Christ," before again shouting, "Ed!!!"

A man's voice yelled back in a Texas drawl. "God damn it, Beverly! What the hell's the matter with you? What do you want?"

She just said, "Door's for you."

The man came to the door and my mother said, "Do you know who I am?"

He mumbled, "Yeah, I know you. How are you?"

Mother said, "I brought your girls to meet you."

"What?!" he roared. "Girls?! Wait! The first one is mine, I know. I don't know who the hell you were foolin' around with, but the other one ain't mine!"

My mother said, "Okay, that's fine, if you say so. Do you want to see Kari?"

"Come on in," he said without enthusiasm.

My mother shoved me through the door first, and then Kari. When my father turned around, he saw me and laughed.

"Well, I guess that one's mine, too," he said.

Mother smirked. "Ya think?"

It was true. I was a dead ringer for my father.

He took us around to meet all the relatives who lived within shouting distance. Before he could even say who I was, different relatives would pipe up and say, "You Ed's boy? Jesus Christ, Ed! Which wife's he from?"

My dad would say, "This is Terri Lee's daughter, my first wife."

"Oh, you're a girl. Well, you look just like him."

For years now, I've been told I look like my father's twin. I have a photograph of him that people swear is me.

After that reunion, I didn't see or hear from my father for years, not until Mother made him take custody of me.

On October 7, 1977, when I was eleven, Mother annulled all her marriages at once. While the judge was granting the annulments, Mother apparently made a smartass comment along the likes of, "Does that include the children?"

The judge replied, "I can clearly see why each and every one of your husbands left you. My advice to you is, save us all a lot of trouble and don't get another one." And with that, he sent her out of the courtroom.

I ran the streets with my friends Rod, Ricky and Buddy while my mother was nowhere to be found. I played in the sewer pipe where no harm could come to me and no one could find me. Rod would sometimes come down there on his bike and try to kiss me. One day he showed me his penis. I was fascinated. "How come I don't have one?"

I became interested in seeing it again and wondered how I could get a penis like that. I just had to have one. Being in a girl's body didn't feel natural to me, let alone the feminine clothes I was forced to wear. I had several moments as a child when I felt almost like I was another person being made to live a lie. My mother wanted so badly for me to just fit in.

My rage started to find different ways to express itself. I began shoplifting, killed small birds, threw rocks at windows and then run. Another trick involved tying string from one tree to another, and then tying it to a tree on the other side of the street. When a car came down the hill, the string pulled the wiper blades off the windshield. My behavior was becoming more and more destructive.

In 1977, one of the boys in class asked me to the opening of *Star Wars*. Who could pass that up? So, I went. Although he tried to hold my hand the entire time, I managed to see the movie and made it home without him getting anywhere.

In 1978, sixth-grade graduation was nearing. I was both relieved yet sad to leave Mr. Rodarte. What would happen now? Each of us were going in different directions. We felt like lost souls forced to deal with the big world on our own after being together in a small class for so long. How would we cope with junior high's multiple classrooms and scads more students and teachers?

At sixth-grade graduation, my mother made me wear a godawful dress. Although I wore a T-shirt and shorts under it, and despite my long hair, I always looked and felt like a boy wearing a dress.

We sang "Memories," by Debby Boone and I stood between Rod and Buddy, who were both trying to hold my hand. We might never see each other again, I figured, so this time I didn't fight them.

After graduation, I stayed in contact with Rod and Ricky for a time, but Rod just wanted to make out with me. Besides the fact that he had bucked teeth, I was never going to kiss a boy even if he had nice teeth. No way, no how.

As time went on and another year passed, things seemed to get only crazier at home. Mother and Glen had reconciled a few times and when she was home, she and Glen were fighting more. It seemed as though she was always screaming about something. I couldn't stand it.

Mother continued to beat us with wire hangers or whatever was within reach. Mother also slapped us, pinched our faces, but the punishments with belts and hangers were the worst. In later years she spoke about how much she admired Joan Crawford. She made us call her Mother Dear or Mother Dearest, and refused to answer unless we did. She even began signing cards and letters that way.

Mother also killed several of our pets by putting them in the dryer or the freezer while still alive. Because I so badly wanted her love and affection, I never reported it. Sometimes Mother would sit in a chair with her arms around me, rocking back and forth, saying, "TJ, now you know I love you. I have always loved you. Y'know that, don't you? But y'know what you do is wrong. Come on, love on Mother."

She would pull me close and try to put my arms around her, but I just couldn't do it. I never knew why she did what she did, but always suspected she had serious mental problems. I know she had major emotional ones.

After Glen left for the last time, Mother picked up where she left off, carousing around and dating many men, one of whom was my grandfather by marriage. We started to go over to my grandmother's house more often. This is when my step-grandfather started to molest me. Sometimes he showed me his penis. Other times he walked around with his robe hanging open, or walked back and forth in front of an open door while naked. If we were alone, he would try to put his hand in my pants or his tongue in my mouth. I would escape by pushing him off and then go find my grandmother. I told my mother, but she didn't do anything.

With Mother becoming increasingly absent, my sister Kari and I were often home alone. Kari became even more sexually active and I was now really starting to struggle with my own sexual identity. I didn't know what was wrong with me. Friends were talking about boys and dating, but not me. I was busy following girls who I had crushes on. I often looked at girls and wondered why I behaved the way I did, because I could see it was not natural.

By the time I was in seventh grade, my attraction to girls was in full swing. I began following one girl around school like a hormonal schoolboy. Her name was Margie, and her locker was near mine. She was tall and wore her blonde hair in a short bob, parted down the middle and feathered back. She always wore tight blue jeans and a shirt.

I suppose Margie was older than me because she had big breasts. And boy, she was hot! One time she got close enough to distract me and I accidently slammed my hand in the locker, jamming a pencil into my hand. How was I going to explain *that* to my mother? What was I going to say? "Oh, by the way, I was checking out a girl and slammed my hand in a locker..."

No way. I had enough problems already. I had to go to the hospital to have the lead removed from the palm of my hand.

My feelings for girls intensified. I rebelled against dresses and female clothing of any kind. It was blue jeans, T-shirts and Wallabies for me. I became your average 1970s dyke.

By this time, my mother was pretty much nowhere to be found. Left to our own devices, my sister Kari and I often went down to the local Square Pan Pizza joint to buy smokes from the machine for fifty cents. We stopped going to church, and Kari started smoking pot. I remember the first time she offered me some. Along with one of her boyfriends, us three all got stoned. Our life was out of control. Not long after, Mother decided we needed to move.

In 1980, I was fourteen when we moved to Fallbrook in northern San Diego county. Mother said we moved because Kari had become sexually out of control and we would have a better life in Fallbrook. In fact, it was the opposite. Fallbrook was known for having the best marijuana around.

We moved from our safe, comfortable three-bedroom, two-bath house with a yard into a three-bedroom, two-bath mobile home in a trailer park located just outside the back gate of Marine Corps Base Camp Pendleton. Mother took a factory job at a place called Robert Shaw Manufacturing. Once again, she was hardly home and we found ourselves running wild in the streets of a small town.

I later learned that when our mother wasn't working, she was meeting our step-grandfather and other men at the bars. This man was my grandfather by marriage, not by birth. So my mother was having an affair with her own mother's second husband. He, in turn, was molesting me. I was far from the only screwed up person in the family.

There was a stretch of time when we didn't see my grandmother and her husband, which wasn't unusual. Mother often went several years without speaking to relatives. When we did see them, the molestation picked up right where it left off.

Eighth grade got off to a rocky start. Now five-foot seven-inches tall and 170 pounds, I was a big girl in a new town. I wore Levi jeans, T-shirts, and hair to my shoulders. I walked into my first class, which happened to be gym. I took my registration card up to the teacher sitting at a desk. She glanced up and said, "You'll need a jock by next class."

I was a little puzzled. I had no idea what she was talking about. Not wanting to feel stupid in front of the kids standing behind me in line, I said quietly, "A what?"

She raised her voice and repeated, "A jock...you know, an athletic supporter. All boys have to have them for P.E."

As the class roared with laughter, I shouted, "Fuck you, bitch! I'm a girl! Can't you see my tits?"

I bolted out of there and ditched school the rest of the day.

From then on, I was marked as the school dyke. All those years of feeling humiliated because I was a girl instead of a boy became more than I could bear. Thoughts of suicide ran rampant in my mind. I had the same conversation with myself over and over. How can I kill myself? I just can't live like this any longer. I hate myself, my body and my mind! Why couldn't I have just been born normal? After one such conversation, I went to the local grocery store and stole a pack of cigarettes— a mild act of defiance compared to what was yet to come.

Some of my friends were class stoners, others were school misfits. Kelly was one true friend and her dad owned the local restaurant. Kelly knew I liked girls. She told me, "Hey TJ, it's okay if you like girls. I'm still your friend."

I completely freaked out and denied it. "What the hell are you talking about? Are you crazy?"

She just laughed and said, "Okay, whatever."

She was right, though. I did like girls. But I didn't like being one. I didn't know anyone else like me, so I still felt like a complete outcast yet Kelly never judged me and remains a friend to this day.

I had a lot of trouble in junior high, and got into fights with both boys and girls. I fought well, and understood the art of fisticuffs. Also known as bare knuckle boxing or fighting, it just felt natural.

One girl in particular kept trying to get a rise from me. During P.E., the girls were made to wear one-piece jumpsuit shorts. Oh, hell, no! I was wearing what the boys wore—gym shirt and shorts. This girl made fun of me every time.

One day while making fun of me, she poked me over and over in the chest. My rage boiled over into a blackout and I let loose. By the time I was done she had a fractured wrist, two broken ribs, broken nose, sprained hand, two black eyes, and a patch of missing hair. She swore that one day she would pay me back. She never did.

A lot of this is like a blur in some ways. Before I knew it, junior high was over. I failed most classes yet somehow passed. Maybe they just didn't want to deal with me anymore and were glad to get rid of me.

By the time high school began, Mother wasn't happy with who I was or how I behaved. I was still punching walls, getting into fights, smoking, and staying out until late at night. She took me for counseling and I tried telling her that I liked girls. She responded, "What you're trying to tell me is that you're a dyke, one of those gays? Yeah, well, I already knew you were queer. You think I am stupid?"

I didn't understand why I was the way I was, and her response didn't make me feel any better. I thought I had multiple personalities at one point, and really just wanted to die.

One day I was tired of being ridiculed and decided to ditch school and go home. As I walked up to the house, I saw a police car parked in front. I went in to see what was happening and found my mother in the living room talking to police. I snuck into my room and shut the door.

A few seconds later, the door flew open and they said, "You're under arrest for theft!"

My mother claimed I had swiped her TV, which she had hidden in a trunk in the living room. I fought the deputy while trying to explain that the TV was in the trunk. My mother was in the background saying, "I'm so sorry, TJ."

She stood there fake crying as I yelled obscenities at her. I now hated her even more. Why was she doing this to me? I was taken away in the patrol car and driven down to the police station. I sat there as they asked me a bunch of questions.

They said my mother told them I had stolen her TV and was out of control. She added that she thought it all stemmed from the fact that I was being molested by my grandfather. In looking back, I have a sick feeling she was jealous that he had done that to me, but at the time all I said was, "I guess what she said is the way it is."

She insisted I press charges against my step-grandfather. Soon after, she instructed me to recant the story. I assume they must have had a falling out and then made up again.

In the meantime I was taken to Hillcrest Receiving Home. I remained there for quite a while, although for how long, I don't know. I do know I hated it there, and saw things I never thought I'd see.

One day my biological father, Ed, came to pick me up. I now had to go live with him in Arizona.

Why was my mother doing this to me? Did she think I would change? Did she think I would stop liking girls?

As we drove down the road, I remember looking in the mirror at my father's eyes, his face and everything about him. Do I really look like this man? Is this who my mother claims I look and act so much like? I studied his face for a long time. He hardly said anything to me over the next several hours.

We arrived in Arizona at the same old rickety trailer he was living in when I first met him. Home sweet home? I guess that was the idea. It didn't last long, though. I started wetting the bed again, which I hadn't done in a long time. Aside from that, I smoked and pretty much did whatever I pleased.

Eventually, Ed's wife called my mother and forced me to say I did not want to be there and wanted to come home. I knew I was unwanted there, so I did. My mother told me I had to tell the police that I lied about my grandfather, and had to apologize to him as well. Only then would she let me come home. I agreed and did what she asked. As a kid, I did what I had to do to survive.

CHAPTER SIX

High school

High school started, and Mother and I seemed to get along at first. My older sister moved in and out of the house, and was living there when I returned from Arizona. It felt like a completely new world for me, and I was glad my sister was there.

High school was the start of discovering myself as gay, or something outside the norm. Because I liked girls, I didn't know what to do with myself. I hated school because I never thought I was smart. My lack of self-esteem was largely fed by the fact that my mother had always put me in special education classes. When I was ridiculed in class, anger would surface. I didn't hesitate to call people filthy names and stalk out of the classroom. It felt like I was on a merry-go-round that always ended up in the office, in detention, or getting suspended.

In retrospect, perhaps it would have been better had I been put in one single class. It reached the point where only one teacher would put up with me.

I hated my body so much and was so embarrassed, there was no way I was going to dress in front of other girls in P.E. when I couldn't even dress in front of myself. I opted to change in and out of my gym clothes in a bathroom stall where nobody could see me. This didn't help my situation, though. Kids made fun of me even more, contributing to a growing inability to function at school.

Mother then had me committed to a halfway house called Oz. It was the next place in the series of places where I was taken because she didn't want to deal with me. The one good thing about Oz, though, was that I was free. I could be myself and was allowed to smoke and hang out. We were free to do pretty much whatever we wanted as long as we helped out around the place and went to counseling.

While there I started menstruating for the first time. Because Mother had never discussed those things with me, I had no clue what was happening. I didn't know what to do. I wasn't bleeding badly, and it lasted for only two days and was then gone. After that, I hardly ever had a menses.

My time at Oz proved to be short-lived like all the other places Mother sent me. Back then, I really wanted to believe that on some level she was trying to help me, not dump me onto someone else.

TJ's 9th grade photo

I wound up moving back in with her but soon was sent to another foster home, this time in Poway. I actually got to stay there for quite some time and met all kinds of lesbians, too. Two of my cousins attended the same high school, which helped. The school had a smoking area on the property, and foster parents bought cigarettes for the kids who smoked. Outside school, I continued hanging out with friends and running the streets.

My foster parents didn't like me. I wet the bed a couple time, and was yelled at. They said it wasn't working out there, so once more I was sent back home to my mom.

Nobody understood my frustration, my anger, and especially not my sexuality. How many counselors and teachers does it take to figure out a student is gender-confused? Didn't those issues exist in the '80s?

Yes, they did. Perhaps it hadn't yet come to light in those big fancy college textbooks. That must have been the case, so to all those who treated me back in those days, I suggest you go get your money back because getting your degree obviously didn't prepare you to deal with someone like me. I had to figure it out on my own.

I was returned to Mother but spent the summer with a babysitter, Mrs. Zumwalt, a kind lady who had three kids of her own and adopted eleven others. The idea must have been that with all that experience with kids, she would surely be able to handle me. I was getting ready to go into my sophomore year of high school, yet stuck with a babysitter. It sucked and I was really hateful but managed to stick out the summer until school began again.

My sophomore year I decided to join the softball team. I heard that's where my kind congregated, and it seemed to be true. A high percentage of the school lesbians were on the team. Finally, girls like me liked me! Even straight girls seemed to like me. They often said, "You act like a guy."

I'd just smile. That made me feel good because that's how I felt. I still wished to be a guy, but the reality was I was a girl. I had no alternative other than to live my life as gay.

I wasn't quite out of the closet yet, because I didn't exactly know what being gay meant. But the town was like hitting a lesbian goldmine. To me, it seemed like every lesbian in the country lived there, and it went without saying that if you played softball, more than likely you were a lesbian.

My sister Kari has played softball ever since we were kids yet wasn't a lesbian herself. I went to one of Kari's games, and that's where I met the woman with whom I would soon have my first encounter.

There were two older sisters who played on Kari's team. One was gay and the other wasn't. The gay sister always talked to Kari, and my sister would say to me, "She's just like you, ya know? She likes girls."

I would pretend I didn't know what she was talking about and tell my sister to fuck off. After games, we went down to the local pizza place with all the players and they'd drink beer and eat pizza.

The gay sister used to call me Diaper Dyke. I hated that yet didn't even know what that meant. She and her girlfriend were more than a little weird. Her girlfriend was heavyset and wore tight jeans. Her blouse was always unbuttoned to expose large breasts, and she had long red fingernails. She wore her hair in an afro style, and her perfume was horrible. She always smiled at me, which gave me the creeps, so I avoided her as much as possible.

I kept going to the games, though, because I developed a crush on the straight sister. She knew it, too, and often flirted with me and made gestures and innuendos. One time when we were at the pizza place after a game, I went to use the bathroom and she followed me. Once in the bathroom, she pushed me into one of the stalls and we started kissing. She was in her late twenties, and I was only fifteen. She and I had a relationship on and off for a few months.

My mother didn't condone my lifestyle, and my behavior was progressively out of control. My grades were falling, I hated school, and hated myself. I continued to think about suicide. I prayed for God to just please help me die, or send me the courage to end my own life. I felt I could no longer live like this. I hated being a freak, a girl, or whatever I was.

My mother thought it would be best if she sought help from the Mormon church. Would an exorcism help? Would it change my wanting to become a guy? Would it force me into wearing a dress and heels, and turn me into a proper young lady? Back to church we went. No way was I going to wear a dress this time. A suit and tie, maybe. Bless her cold heart.

My mother went to the church bishop and told him I was homosexual, uncontrollable, and needed help. Consequently, I was removed from my mother's home and the church temporarily placed me with a family who owned a local feed store until a more suitable family could be found. It turned out that none were available or willing to take me. The bishop had nine children of his own, and agreed to take me in as a foster child, making their family my second official foster home. It was excruciatingly painful.

I attended bible study every morning before school, a class for young adults on Wednesdays, and church on Sundays. I hated it. I wasn't allowed to smoke, see my friends, and it went without saying that I must refrain from homosexual activity.

I snuck out and smoked every chance I got. I got the best pot from the girls at church but when they got caught, I was to blame. I was an easy target and they couldn't pass up using me as a scapegoat. Once again I was asked to leave.

Back to Mother's I went, and she was not happy about it. We tried to get along but within a few weeks it was back to where we started. All the fighting and screaming, just like always. Why couldn't she see what was happening to me?

It seemed like the best solution was to just keep searching for ways to kill myself. I hated me, anyway—my body, my breasts, everything. If I had just been born a boy, none of this would be happening.

What kind of sick joke had God played on me? When I used public restrooms, women would say, "Hey, what is the matter? Can't you read? You're in a women's bathroom!"

Someone once called the police and I was asked to prove I was a girl. After that, I never used a women's bathroom again. I learned to hold my urine for hours.

I continued to get into fights with both boys and girls, but managed to stay in school and start the tenth grade. By this time it seemed as though a huge influx of lesbians had descended on the school. In looking back, I think I had just begun to notice them is all.

Lesbians were suddenly everywhere. The outfit of choice was Levi 501s, Van's tennis shoes, T-shirts and baseball caps. The car of choice was a Datsun 280z. The favorite hangout were the gym lockers near the P.E. teachers, to accommodate the students and teachers who were dating one another.

I met my friend Alice through my sister, Kari. They were in the same grade, and I had classes with Alice's sister. Despite our three-year age difference, Alice and I became good friends. She seemed to understand me like no one else. I went over to her house nearly every day after school. She helped me with my homework, and her mother was really kind. I started to stay over there until I finally just stopped going home.

I got a job in the butcher shop where Alice worked after school. I kept my grades up, and Mother never asked where I was. For once, life didn't totally suck. One day Alice asked me, "You like girls?"

"Yeah," I answered.

She persisted, "No, I mean *like* girls. Like, *like* them, you know? Like you would guys? I'm asking, because *I'm* gay."

Yes! Finally! Someone like me.

"Yes," I repeated, "Me, too. I do like girls."

After that, we laughed and drove down the road checking out chicks together. Her mother allowed Alice to be open and live freely. Alice even had a girlfriend. I finally didn't feel alone.

In many ways, I felt more alive than I ever had, yet something still wasn't right. I still didn't feel normal. I continued to feel depressed yet didn't know why. How could this be? I had finally discovered I was gay and had relationships with women yet something still felt wrong.

While still in high school, I met Mike, a gay boy my age. We frequented the gay club scene in and around San Diego, and dabbled in drugs together along with other illegal activeities. I'm not proud of those things and never got caught, thank god. I was staying out all hours of the night and soon met my first drag queens. I had never seen a transvestite before and was mesmerized by all the men who loved to dress like women. Thinking I was a guy, many tried to pick me up. When they discovered I wasn't male, they continued to flirt and I became friends with some.

Although it was a freeing time, I remained confused about my own sexuality. I couldn't figure out why men could become women, but women couldn't become men. This fueled inner frustration, and my thoughts of suicide continued to grow.

CHAPTER SEVEN

Takin' care of Business

Alice was a mothering type, and when she learned of what I was doing in San Diego, she came to get me. She was pissed, and laid down the law that she was not going to let me keep going down the wrong path. I was only seventeen, and knew she had my best interests at heart. I returned to Fallbrook to live with Alice and went back to school.

One of my teachers set me up for a summer job interview. No ifs, ands, or buts. I was going to attend that interview. The teacher even arranged a ride for me. She handed me the application and asked, "Do you need help filling it out?"

The application was for a job with the California Department of Forestry. I looked it over, completed it, and then went to the interview. While waiting to graduate from high school, I received a letter saying I had been accepted into the state forestry's fire academy. The letter explained that training was forty hours per week, and outlined everything I needed to get going. My grandmother took me to buy all the things I would need for the academy. This is how my career as a firefighter started. It didn't change the fact that I was still obviously a girl.

I now had everything. A great job, my own car, and girls who liked me. But there was still something drastically wrong. I continued to hate myself, and had a deep need to be someone else. On the outside I appeared to be a happy, funny, and fun-loving person. Yet on the inside I was suicidal, angry, hateful and incredibly frustrated. It felt as though I could explode at any moment, yet nobody could see it except me.

I was in therapy at the time, yet still afraid to say what was truthfully on my mind. If I did, I feared they would put me in a mental hospital and throw away the key.

My friends encouraged me to just accept who I was. Some recommended I try wearing a strap-on penis, which seemed creepy. Others advised I undergo a double mastectomy. While that was a valid option, I assumed no doctor would perform that without a medical reason.

I couldn't look at myself from the neck down. How could I be intimate with someone if I couldn't look at my own body? When I tried to be intimate, I had to keep my shirt on and no one could touch me. I couldn't live like that.

Straight girls wanted a penis, so I finally bought one. It did make things easier and felt natural, yet I wanted my own. As I grew older, I became more frustrated. I wanted to be a man yet needed to maintain some sort of normalcy.

I dabbled in drugs and alcohol for a short time but was afraid of the consequences. So I smoked cigarettes, and traded drugs and alcohol for bulimia. Maybe I could puke or starve my way to death. On the surface, people thought I was happy and had a good life. What they didn't know was that behind closed doors I was a suicidal, bulimic, gender-confused person still looking for the courage to kill myself.

I worked for the California Department of Forestry for two years. By then I was in my early twenties, living life pretty much on my own. I switched over to the U.S. Forest Service but remained a seasonal firefighter for the state of California. The Forest Service had a better reputation than the state, and I liked it better because I worked with more lesbians.

I didn't have a steady girlfriend. Although several girls were interested in me, I found it just too difficult to explain to them how I felt. Instead I dated several girls, not allowing myself to get too serious about any particular one.

I moved around from place to place, and acted out my gender crisis by remaining unsettled in virtually every area of my life. I continued to be ridiculed, and was often called sir, a guy, dyke, queer, homo, take your pick. It didn't matter whether my hair was long or short. Women still assumed I couldn't read signs before entering public restrooms.

Whenever I bought tampons, the store clerk would say, "Sir, your girlfriend or wife must be lucky to have you. My boyfriend certainly would never do that for me!"

I'd reply, "Well, they probably don't have their period, either, do they?"

I would laugh and walk away, saying, "Can't you see the tits? Now who can't see?"

Inside it was killing me. I really wanted to punch them in the face. People are so blatantly rude. Why do people have to say anything at all? What if it was you or your child? How would you feel if someone said that to you or them?

Maybe joining the military would solve my problems. I was about twenty-one when I visited an army recruiter who took me to San Diego's Military Entrance Processing Station to take the Armed Services Vocational Aptitude Battery, a multi-aptitude test. An older, heavyset man, the recruiter told me I was a little overweight and would have to get my body fat down but not to worry, he could help me do that.

I soon learned he wanted to help me do that in more ways than one. Put it this way, it wasn't just him that was standing at attention. He said he could transform me before I went into the service, and reassured me that once I had his cock, I would never want another woman. Thanks, but no thanks.

He knew I was gay. Did he think he was going to give me a rooster and suddenly I would turn into a man and could join the army? Needless to say, I never went back to his office and I never went into the army.

I continued to work for the forestry service. It was a good job that paid well. During the off season, I worked odd jobs or went to school. Despite a full life, I remained depressed, suicidal, and felt totally hopeless. I didn't know where to turn.

By this time, I had seen several therapists yet not one had mentioned sex reassignment surgery. They told me I had bipolar, anger issues, depression, and/or an eating disorder, and should try Al-Anon, OA, sex addiction or some other support group. Eager to find a way to reconcile who I was, I tried them all. Still nothing. I was resigned to trying to accept me for me.

Now that I was twenty-one and legally allowed to go to bars, a whole new world opened up. I was frequenting one such bar in San Diego, where I became friends with the bartender, Linda E.

TJ with friend Linda E.

I was now five-foot-nine, tan with brown-blonde hair and blue eyes and had become what Linda E. called androgynous. I wore a black leather jacket with a cock ring on the shoulder, white T-shirt, black Levi jeans and black boots, Doc Martens. I landed a part-time job working the front door of the bar. I still worked as a firefighter and even had a girlfriend who was attending a nearby police academy. We dated on and off for two years though she wasn't very faithful during our relationship.

Looking back, every relationship I had was dysfunctional. I was so confused about who I was, and never felt comfortable in my own skin. It's hard to have a good relationship when you can't look at yourself, let alone like yourself.

I remained desperate to understand what was wrong with me. I didn't feel like I was gay, yet liked girls and didn't like men. What was I? I didn't fit in anywhere.

Why could men become women yet women couldn't become men? Although it took many years, I was getting closer to figuring myself out. But for the time being, I continued to run from my problems in hopes they would just disappear.

I decided to pursue a full-time job as a firefighter. About this same time, I met Katie, an engineer for Poway City. She encouraged me to take her fire department's test. I took both the written and physical agility tests, and was the only female to pass the seven-minute test in 4 minutes, 44 seconds. I also beat a lot of the men.

Despite all that, I was becoming obsessed with thoughts of wanting to become a man. My depression was worsening and I felt myself sinking deeper. Life wasn't fair.

Once again I decided that what I really needed was to get away. So at age twenty-three, I took the Navy's entrance exam. I scored high enough to go to dental school, so selected dental school as a billet. I was assigned to bootcamp in Florida.

Following bootcamp, I would return to San Diego for school and then to Holy Loch, Scotland, for four years. I was stoked and passed everything easily, but then was asked one question.

"Are you a homosexual?"

"No!" I said.

"Okay," the guy said, "Sign here."

Second question. "Have you ever smoked pot?"

I thought about this one for a moment. I didn't want to lie because I figured most people probably lied, but he'll know I wasn't telling the truth. So, I answered, "Yes!"

He shook his head. "Oh, well you can't have dental school because of that, or be in the medical field."

My heart stopped for a moment. He then said, "We do have one rate open. Firefighter. If you want it, you'll have to wait until it opens in July to go. If not, you'll have to wait until a rate that you want opens."

"Okay, I'll take it."

And with that I became a Navy firefighter. I continued working for the state forestry service as a seasonal firefighter until I entered the Navy on July 17, 1989. I was twenty-three years-old.

TJ's Navy photo (1989).

Before leaving, I buzzed my hair into a flattop. Mother said, "You have done all the things in life I have ever wanted to do. I'm so proud of you!"

As much as I wanted to believe what she said, her words rang hollow. I felt nothing when she hugged me the same way she had when I was a child. I just said goodbye and was on my way. Although it felt a little scary, it mostly felt really good to be leaving.

The night before catching the plane to bootcamp, we had to stay in a hotel. There were two other girls and two guys, and we had to share rooms. I walked into the girls' room, and one girl said, "Hey! This is the girls' hotel room."

I explained that I *was* a girl and assigned to share this room with her. She apologized for thinking I was a guy, and we wound up in the same bootcamp company.

I chain-smoked the entire flight, which was still legal back then. We landed in Orlando, and I didn't know what to expect. I was ushered to the side where the guys were, and thought, oh, crap. For fuck's sake, can't you see the tits? I corrected them and held my temper, and was placed with the girls. I was then led to a berthing area where girls were standing. Someone said, "This is the girls' berthing."

At this point, I was ready to kick someone's ass. I said, "No shit, bitch!"

Some girls were crying, and I tried to calm them down. "This is just a mind game, don't let them get to you."

I then added a few words of sarcasm, and just as the words flew from my mouth, in walked our company commander. In a southern drawl, she said, "Yah think this is a joke? Yah think this is funny?"

I just stood there.

"Good. Then you can be my master-at-arms," she said.

I had no clue what she was talking about but was about to find out. Master-at-arms is third in command, and oversees section leaders—the police of the squad. Our company commander, CC, as we called her, was quite the bitch.

When I discovered we had to take open bay showers each morning, I thought, *no way*. I couldn't. How was I going to pull this off for thirteen weeks? I couldn't let anyone see me naked, or shower with all these girls. It would be like a guy without normal body parts bathing with a bunch of women.

TJ with his company commander (1991).

I was determined to lay awake to ensure I would be up before everyone else to shower first. When I realized I couldn't keep doing that, I showered at night which turned out to be much better. I always applied aftershave and some of the girls

74

would come over and say, "I had to smell you before I went to sleep. It reminds me of my boyfriend!"

Then they'd giggle and run off to their bunk. Of course, every time that happened, I fell asleep with a smile. I had good-looking girls in my company.

We were fitted for uniforms I hated. I was sure our CC knew, or at least could tell, I was gay. This was long before the don't-ask-don't-tell rule, though, and she never said a word. While getting fitted, we had to try on long and short skirts. I flipped out. Our CC thought it was hilarious and ordered me to try it on. "Master-at-arms, try that skirt on," she laughed.

I felt and looked like a boy wearing a dress complete with granny heels, military purse and hat. Thank god that uniform was optional. I never wore it and lied to get out of wearing it.

Official photos required that all women wear a skirt. On picture day, I pretended like I hadn't remembered and showed up in dress whites—pants. No way was I going to wear a dress. And when it came time for haircuts, I wasn't allowed to get one. CC ordered me to grow my hair out because I looked like a boy. That was my whole point. She just laughed.

I was strong, athletic, and didn't take shit from anyone. CC even took me over to the male company as an example of a real master-at-arms. She was a bitch, and I loved her for it.

I was selected to swim early in the morning for a chance to be a Navy diver, per our CC's recommendation. I won the athletic award in bootcamp as well. But I had a silent secret no one knew about. I was still unhappy, and still bulimic.

My mind ruminated thoughts of struggling to stay alive, wanting to become a male, trying to suppress suicidal thoughts all the while maintaining a happy exterior. It was so hard and exhausting but I had to keep moving forward.

I graduated bootcamp, and Mother and her new husband came to watch. I said goodbye to my company commander, a woman who never once judged me for who I was. We remain in contact to this day. She is and has always been a wonderful addition to my life.

I went home on leave before school started, and then returned to Florida for school instead of San Diego. By this time, I had met a girl who at first thought I was a sailor guy. We hit it off right away, and hung out with each other and friends in our time off. She continued to flirt with me and we eventually became involved. I didn't think it would last very long, knowing we would have to part ways once we received our orders.

I was being sent to Virginia instead of Scotland, which I wasn't thrilled about but had no choice. I soon said goodbye, and off I went to my duty station.

Arriving in Virginia, I had never been near a Navy ship, let alone onboard one. With seabag on my back and suitcase in hand, I trucked down the pier in my Navy dress. God, I felt stupid, like everyone was staring at me. I reported in, and a big, burly woman with a lot of tattoos came to get me. She said, "I'll show you where your rack is."

The ship was filled with lesbians and for the first time in my life I felt right at home. I laughed to myself that I had been stationed on the USS Lesbian with the motto, "We sail any where!" Who would've thought?

Most of the lesbians appeared as manly as I was. The rest were considered the skanks. I settled in pretty well and made friends fast.

One friend, Nancy, was from San Diego, too. Eventually she and I decided to move off base and get an apartment. I had a girlfriend aboard the ship who worked in the photolab, and she often stayed at our place.

Nancy never had a girlfriend. She was a big girl, and even though that shouldn't have made a difference, the Navy looked for reasons to get rid of Nancy because of her size. She was a great person, and for them to do that was very unfair.

One day, Nancy said there was a new girl onboard who she liked. She was pretty sure the girl liked her, too. Feeling pretty confident the new girl was gay, Nancy planned to ask her out. She added, "You better not fuck it up for me."

As mentioned, Nancy was a big girl, especially from the waist down. But I was quite the ladies' lady. Every time Nancy found a girl she liked, they end up liking me instead of Nancy.

Since we lived off base and shared an apartment, well, I couldn't help it if Nancy's girls liked me. Most of them weren't my type though, and I already had a girlfriend.

Nancy wanted to introduce me to this new girl on the ship instead of at our apartment, just to be safe. I agreed to meet them in our berth, our living space on the ship. I was having a smoke when Nancy stepped through the hatch and said, "TJ, here she is. I want you to meet Misty."

I couldn't see Misty at first because Nancy's large figure filled the door. And then there she was. At 4' 10", with short blonde hair and blue eyes, she was the cutest thing I ever saw. At eighteen years-old, she giggled the same time she said hello.

I had no idea whether Misty liked me, but from the first moment I saw her I was smitten. Because of Nancy, though, I played it cool. Misty later told me she thought I was an ass, but I grew on her as time went by, and we became good friends. Today, Misty and I are married.

At the time, I already had a girlfriend. Misty actually hated her and to tell the truth, by that time, so did I. I would much rather have been with Misty, but she was straight. Nancy was very disappointed to learn this, but not nearly as much as I was.

The Navy finally succeeded in drumming poor Nancy out of the service, basing their decision on her physical size and what they said was her unhealthiness. I've haven't heard from her since she left, but Misty and I have talked about Nancy and hope she's happy, wherever she landed.

Even though I knew Misty was straight, she was so special to me. I was determined to hold onto her as a friend, if nothing else. She always punched me when she walked by, so everyone thought we had something going on. Always together, one of our supervisors called us Butch and Sundance.

Misty's boyfriend hated me. She ended up marrying him, even though I told her not to. As it turns out, if she hadn't, then there would have been no big brother for my son.

Even though Misty and I enjoyed great times together, I remained quite depressed. Every day was a struggle. If only I was a man, life would be so simple. I felt miserable yet couldn't explain to anyone the anxiety or frustration I felt. I found myself wishing someone would kill me, and envisioned my own death and funeral, even the people who would be there.

Something inside me just wasn't right. I felt I was going out of my mind, becoming more withdrawn from people, and angry. It was as if another person was living inside my mind at times. Why couldn't I just be normal?

I drove myself crazy, wondering whether I was straight, gay or asexual. I was so confused. I liked women but didn't feel gay. I didn't want to be with men because that felt abnormal. Nothing felt normal. I finally couldn't take it any longer and decided to put an end to my misery. The next morning I took a bottle of sleeping pills. I could no longer live in this body or mind. I could no longer live in this body of mine.

I almost escaped, but not quite. Misty and our senior chief knew something was wrong when I failed to report for duty on the ship at 7:30 a.m. They came to check on me and called 911. Charcoal was pumped into my stomach and I was transported to Port Smith Naval Hospital. I was sent to the psych ward for a forty-eight-hour evaluation. What was I going to do now? I was alive. I had failed.

How was I going to explain myself? I knew that telling the truth would ruin my Navy career so I lied, chalked it up to stress and said it wouldn't happen again. In my heart of hearts, I just wanted to become a man—it was the only way I could tolerate the thought of living.

While in the psych ward, flashbacks of being institution-alized as a child fueled my anger. I was released after forty-eight hours and sent home with a clean bill of mental health. I had fooled everybody yet again.

Eventually I left Virginia and was stationed close to home. I attended Navy dive school, and they promised to send me to Hawaii. I agreed, and took the change. I said goodbye to Misty and my other friends, and me and my belongings drove back to California. I would miss Misty greatly and hoped we would keep in touch. Even though her husband didn't like me, she was a dear friend, and I loved her.

I arrived at Naval Station Point Loma in San Diego, and started electrician school to become a Seabee. I would then go on to dive school in Hawaii. I was glad to be back in my home-town with friends, yet a big piece of my life remained missing.

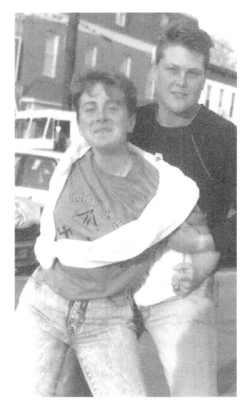

Misty (18) and TJ (24).

CHAPTER EIGHT

Where there's smoke . . .

On July 17, 1991, I was discharged from the Navy for homosexuality. It was no big deal like it's often made out to be. Some guy approached me and said, "Are you Terry Barganski?"

"Yes," I replied.

"You're being discharged as per the UCMJ Military Justice Code with an RE-4 Honorable for the crime of homosexuality-bisexuality," he rattled. "Do you understand?"

"Yes," I said again. And with that I was dismissed.

An RE-4 meant I could never reenlist in the military. The don't-ask-don't-tell policy was issued December 1993. Maybe they had a quota of how many lesbians they needed to cut before that went into effect, and I just got caught in the net.

The Forest Service gave me my job back, and I was sent to Cottonwood Ranger Station. I got a small apartment down from the bar where I used to work. It was all good except my depression was getting worse and thoughts of suicide were ever present.

It always came back to the same old question—why can't women become men? I still had no idea they could. I never mentioned wanting or needing to do this to anyone, so my frustration continued to mount every day

After work I became more isolated, more bulimic, and slimmer. I continued to work and act like nothing was wrong in my life. People saw me as a happy, healthy individual who would help anyone.

I hung at the bar where my friend Linda E. still worked. I felt comfortable talking to her. We had a strange connection and she seemed to understand me on a level others didn't. She was a very spiritual person who was more in tune with what was going on in the world. We were told once that we were brothers in a past life.

Perhaps I had been a man in all my previous incarnations, and just journeyed to this life in the first vessel I found, which happened to be a female body. What was I thinking?

I stayed with the Forest Service and applied for a full-time position. While waiting, I was called to interview with the federal fire department. I went dressed in a blazer, jeans and, of course, short hair. The fire chief was a rather large man who seemed quite nice during the interview.

"Sit down, young man," he said.

I didn't say anything or correct him. I figured he'd look at the application and discover his Freudian slip. He continued to interview me but said nothing more regarding gender. At the end of the interview he said, "We will contact you if you are selected as a new hire," and that was it.

I was contacted a short time later and in August 1991, began my career as a federal firefighter. While completing my new hire paperwork, I noticed some areas had *male* checked. I wondered if perhaps they thought they hired a male. Whatever the case, it was too late now. I was hired on and starting a new phase in my life.

I started my federal fire department job in San Diego. I went all out, totally gung-ho. I was hired along with several other males. No other females were hired or went through the academy at the same time we did. My mother and her current husband showed up for my graduation, and after that I was sent to the 32nd Street fire station.

I was the only female at the station and although I felt intimidated, I wasn't about to show it. Everyone called me the FNG, for fuckin' new guy. It went without saying that I would have to prove myself. Not only was I one of two newbies on probation, they saw me as a gay female. I got such dirty looks from the other firefighters that if

TJ (1991).

looks could kill, I would have dropped dead that first week.

One of the firefighters said, "We aren't used to females here, and the guys sleep in their underwear. Hope that doesn't offend you."

"Why would it?" I asked.

He snorted, "Well, in case you see something you aren't used to seeing."

I said, "It's not often I carry a pocket magnifying glass searching for small objects in the dark, so I doubt if I will find anything. But if I come across something that offends me, I'll be sure to let you know." He never spoke to me again.

My first night at the station, the bells went off when a structure fire was reported. I was both excited and scared. Although I was used to brushfires, I was ready to roll and take on whatever was waiting for me. In retrospect, it was like one of those old deodorant commercials—never let 'em see you sweat.

I jumped into my bunker gear and down the pole I went. Our firehouse had a brush engine, fire engine, and firetruck. Both the fire engine and firetruck were dispatched. I was on the fire engine and although it wasn't my first fire, it was my first structure fire. Yet, I was on top of my game, and did just what I was supposed to do.

My captain was impressed and told me, "Good job!"

I wondered what they expected from a lesbian. Did they think I was weak and frail? Come on!

On the other hand, the other newbie seemed to have lost his way and had no clue what he was doing. I wondered, when they needed someone to save their life, would they have asked the guy running in circles or the lesbian who did a good job?

They didn't like that I was a lesbian.

There was only one shower in the main station, and eventually I had to use it. They said to make sure I looked at the sign before entering the bathroom so I would know whether guys were in there showering. I was to do the same when I showered but not when I used the bathroom? Guess that didn't matter as much because the stalls had doors. The shower, however, was an open bay with four showerheads.

One day I had the sign up indicating I was showering, and could hear the other firefighters laughing and talking. I didn't know exactly what was going on, but it made me nervous. I assumed that a firehouse was a safe place and nothing would happen. I was mistaken.

Next thing I heard was, "Okay, Chief, be careful," and in walked a prevention chief wearing nothing but his underwear. Before I said anything, he realized what was going on. "Oh, shit! Sorry, man," he said, and turned around and left.

Everyone was laughing. "Hey, we were just fuckin' with you. All probes go through it."

I had experienced my fair share of verbal harassment over the years, but this was the first time I had been intentionally set up. I felt uncomfortable on an entirely new level.

I couldn't stand the pressure and was beginning to feel as though I was losing my mind again. Just when I thought I had found happiness, I found myself back to the same rumination of wanting to become a man.

What was wrong with me? I kept telling myself that I had it all—a girlfriend, a job, an apartment, a car, friends. So, what was my problem? Why was I tormenting myself with thoughts of wanting to become a man? Why can't I just have a normal brain and be happy?

I went to a therapist again to find out what was wrong with me, and was sent to another therapist. And then another. Now according to all these geniuses, I needed Prozac because I was depressed. Or maybe I should really be on Depakote for bipolar. When I had trouble with insomnia, it was, "Here, have some Trazodone."

Or, "Got anxiety, TJ? Try Neurontin."

With all those medications, I thought to myself, for fuck's sake, these people went to school and got advanced degrees. I had told them each the same story. How do you get so many different diagnoses with the same story?

Finally, let's not forget anger. It was determined I needed anger management. Yes, I was angry. Who the hell wouldn't be after all those diagnoses? Yes, I needed anger management from seeing all those therapists and trying to absorb and deal with all the different diagnoses and medications.

On top of that, my bingeing and purging was spiraling out of control. I finally started seeing a therapist for bulimia.

With a growing obsession about wanting to become a man, it felt like there was no hope in sight. To everyone else, it seemed as though I had life together. Yet internally I didn't know up from down. I was sad, angry, confused, and lonely. My inside didn't match my outside at all, and I felt like a damn freak. It was apparent that life was always going to be like this, and I couldn't bear the thought of being doomed to live such misery. Suicidal ideation grew, and this next time around I expected to be successful.

One day at the station, I was laying in my rack watching TV with a buddy. I guess I had contemplated all this too much on my own over the years, and something made me reach out to him. "What would you do if I became a man one day?"

He looked over at me and started laughing. "Really?" he chortled. "You're kidding, right?"

He saw that I wasn't laughing, so he coughed and searched for something else to say. "Shit, I don't care if you turn yourself into a giraffe. As long as you do your job, what would I care?"

For the first time, I dared to think that when it really came down to it, who honestly would care? It turns out they did.

At my very next shift, I was paged over the loudspeaker. "Barganski to the captain's office, on the double."

Shit! What the hell did I do now?

The chief started out by saying, "Sit down." He cleared his throat and continued, "There has been some talk going around the station. Now, it's no secret you know you're open about, well, er, ahm...."

Hell, just like the teachers back in grade school who were nervous about pronouncing Tejai. I decided to throw him a bone to help the guy get off the hook a little bit, just as I had helped those teachers' botched pronunciation of my name.

"You're talking about the fact that I'm gay. Right, sir?"

"Yes, precisely."

He nervously cleared his throat again before plunging forward. "I hear the guys complaining and talking about you, saying you're going to have some sort of sex change or something. Is that true?"

"No. I'm not sure what you're trying to get at here, Chief."

I maintained a calm exterior, but this was starting to feel a lot like my discharge from the Navy. I didn't like where it was heading.

He pushed some papers around on his desk to avoid making eye contact. He finished his speech by saying, "Well, it's just that if you're going to do something like that, please let us know. Otherwise this needs to stop, because it's out of control, and it's making people upset and nervous."

I didn't know what to do. What was the big deal? These big tough firefighters were suddenly upset and nervous? What the hell? Why should they care?

Their teasing was tormenting. "So hey, when are you going to get your add-a-dick-to-me? If you had a real dick, you'd be like that in the first place."

Stupid commentary. The more they disrespected me, the more I disrespected them. Who did they think they were? This was none of their damned business. As long as I did my job and pulled my weight, what difference should it make what kind of plumbing I was equipped with? Besides, I had posed the question to just one buddy, trusting him to answer me honestly. When did everybody else stick their nose into this issue?

Shift after shift, I listened to their ridicule. It was relentless. I wished I had never opened my big mouth. Obviously, nobody could be trusted with this subject; it would always be taboo. All this only served to convince me that I was even more of an aberration. I decided to end it once and for all.

On my way home, I stopped at the drugstore and bought three bottles of sleeping pills. Next stop was a doughnut shop where I bought two blueberry-apple fritters. My final stop was at Roberto's Restaurant for twelve rolled tacos. Might as well enjoy my last supper.

I got home, changed my clothes, shut all my windows and locked my doors. My master plan was in two parts. The first part involved eating all the goodies and then make myself barf so the food wouldn't slow down the effects of the pills. The second part involved swallowing all the sleeping pills, nod off and never wake up again, at least not in this realm. Wherever I wound up had to be better than this living hell.

That was the best plan I could come up with to put the torture of living a lie to rest for good.

I planned to watch TV while eating my last supper. I loved talk shows and it was almost time for Geraldo Rivera. I initialized my master plan and started to eat. The show began and when they introduced the first guest, I stopped eating, frozen in place. I couldn't believe my ears.

"Today our guest is a man who was born biologically a woman, and had surgery to become a man."

I don't remember any alarm bells sending me the signal to abort the master plan. I just know that for a moment I was too stunned to move.

What were the odds that this particular guest would be on at this exact moment? Maybe I did have a guardian angel after all. I grabbed a pen and paper, ready to jot down any important information, and turned up the TV to be sure I didn't miss anything. In retrospect, the blasting volume may have helped convince me that this was real and not a figment of my imagination. I was riveted, listening to every detail. On some level, I believe it was divine intervention.

The guest was in his fifties. I was only in my twenties. I'd been asking people, albeit prescription-happy therapists for the most part, about this kind of surgery for years. Why hadn't anyone mentioned this to me before?

Given the man's age and length of time since his surgery, this option had existed someplace, somewhere, and for quite some time. Was it an underground surgery performed only in dark alleys? Maybe it was some kind of bizarre game therapists played with us, like how many therapists does it takes to find out where to get a sex change in San Diego.

I envisioned their role in the game went something like this. "Oh, let's see. How long should we let our patient think she's gender-confused or crazy before we tell her where to go to get a sex change? Or maybe it would be simpler to just let her kill herself."

I wondered how many other patients had suffered at the hands of a therapist's ignorance, or successfully died by suicide, or been committed to an insane asylum. Or maybe the suggestion of sex reassignment surgery depended upon the patient's economic status.

All these questions flooded my mind as my own personal holy grail unfolded right in front of my eyes on the Geraldo Rivera show. It was nothing short of a miracle, given the fact that I had turned on the TV just in time to stop me from cashing in my chips for good.

I wrote down all the information this wonderful guest had shared, and that same day I started making calls. Come to find out, the doctor who did that guest's surgery no longer practiced, but reaching out and asking questions of qualified, informed people (thank god, they *i* exist!) did lead me to several doctors who currently performed the procedure.

Forget about the last supper and my bulimic plan. I was like a different person—one who had finally been given hope.

I called UCLA, Canada, Virginia, and New York. I spoke to anyone and everyone I could. I even contacted the Geraldo Rivera show to see if I could get in touch with the guest. They agreed, I did, and he called me three weeks later. It turned out he lived only three miles from my house, and we arranged to meet in person. I'll always be grateful to him, and to whoever or whatever orchestrated me turning on the TV at that exact moment. After years of praying and feeling like nobody was listening, or even cared about what might happen to me, my faith was restored by that divine intervention.

Through a series of phone calls and inquiries, I was ultimately directed to Dr. Stanley Biber who was located in Trinidad, Colorado, a thousand miles from San Diego. I was told that Dr. Biber was one of the most renowned sex-change surgeons in the world. Was this the beginning of a life I could actually live with? Hoping for that outcome, I took the leap of faith and called Dr. Biber's office.

CHAPTER NINE

Doctor, doctor, give me the news

The woman who answered Dr. Biber's phone was named Marie, and she said she would send me the Harry Benjamin criteria for female-to-male gender reconstruction. Dr. Harry Benjamin had been an endocrinologist and sexologist who was widely known for his clinical work with transgender people.

I received the information from Marie and studied everything it entailed with more interest than anything I had ever learned in school. It boiled down to this:

- I had to live, dress and work as the opposite sex for one year.

- I must receive hormone therapy for one year before surgery.

- They needed my height, weight, social history and a photo for their files.

- I needed to start working with a certified psychologist, psychiatrist or psychiatric clinician who deals with the treatment of persons in the transgender orientation field.

- I was required to undergo genital hair removal via at least three hundred hours of electrolysis.

- Mandatory HIV testing no later than six weeks prior to surgery.

- They required a $500 deposit.

I had no problem with most of the requirements, but the electrolysis made me a bit nervous. It wasn't the most pleasant part of the program, but the end result would be worth it.

The real stumbling block was how much this was all going to cost, and how I was going to come up with the money. I wanted to do a little research to thoroughly understand what I was proposing to pay for. I wanted to get my money's worth.

The procedure cost at that time was $22,895. It required three trips to Colorado, which cost an additional $1,956 for travel and hotel but didn't include food for the three one-week stays. This also didn't include the mandatory therapy or electrolysis. Insurance considered it an elective surgery and denied coverage. It was immediately apparent I had quite a lot of work to do to prepare for all this, and it wasn't going to be easy.

First, I had to tell my boss. Second, I needed a therapist who wouldn't jack me around. Third, I needed more money which meant a second job. Fourth, I needed to begin undergoing electrolysis.

I didn't know how I was going to do it all nor afford it all, but I did know I was going to go forward with it. I could no longer live the way I'd been existing, as that wasn't living. I was just going through the motions and doing what I had to do to get through each day, feeling incredibly unhappy the entire time. I couldn't take it anymore. The way I saw it, it was really a life or death situation.

I started seeing the eating disorder therapist again, who seemed glad to see me. Her name was Teri Tilker, and at first I wasn't forthcoming about why I had returned, although I did admit I was still vomiting daily. It was a relief to be there, and we started weekly sessions. At about the third week, I told her the truth. "I want to have a sex change."

She didn't look shocked or anything. It was the first time in my life I had said those words, and it was if I had set myself free. I was twenty-seven years old, and for the first time my inner soul felt lifted of the burden I had carried all those years. It was as though someone had cut the ball and chain off my ankle and released me from years of solitary confinement.

A lifetime of sorrow and pain flooded my emotions, and I began to cry uncontrollably. Teri sat beside me in silence. She held and patted my hand, and told me it would be okay, just to let it out.

As I caught my breath and got a hold on myself, I began to laugh and cry simultaneously, saying, "I'm sorry. You must think I'm crazy!"

"Well, I've had one other patient transgender before, so no problem. I'm familiar with the Harry Benjamin procedure," she said.

We kept talking. Thank god she was the right person for me to work with, and already familiar with what I was about to embark upon.

Although Teri remained my therapist throughout the transition, I left her office that day and haven't felt the need to vomit since. A wonderful therapist on many levels, she wrote all the letters required for my procedures, and even appeared on talk shows and news interviews alongside me.

Teri helped the firefighters integrate with the change as well. She was a great deal of help, and an incredible person. I've never forgotten that she was the only therapist who never tried to medicate me. She just listened and helped me with spiritual advice. I will always be grateful.

The next step was locating a doctor to manage the hormone therapy. I started with my primary doctor. She had known my history for some time now, and wasn't surprised at my decision. I was then referred to Dr. Gold, an endocrinologist in San Diego who saw transgender patents. I made an appointment and his only requirements from me as his patient was a letter from Dr. Biber stating I was going to be a transgender patient, and a letter from my therapist stating I was mentally competent. With those in hand, the next phase involved blood tests. As long as those were normal, Dr. Gold was happy to start me on hormone treatment. He gave me information on testosterone and prepared me for side effects.

I left his office and felt one step closer to my new life. Each day seemed better than the last. I felt as though nothing could stop me at this point, but of course, I hadn't yet told any friends or colleagues about my secret plan.

Those closest to me witnessed my transformation from deep depression to hope. Or maybe they thought I was finally on really good mental health drugs. Or just plain good old drugs. I didn't really know what people were thinking until later. For the moment, it was just a huge relief to hope that I might, for the first time in life, really be happy.

12% of adults ages 18-34 identify as
transgender or gender non-conforming.

HARRIS POLL (2017)

CHAPTER TEN

Needling in more ways than one

My next step was to seek out electrolysis, a method of removing individual hairs from the body. This was not going to be fun. Just the act of electrolysis was frightening, let alone trying to find a technician who was licensed to perform the exact type I required.

Electrolysis had become pretty popular, as it eliminated the need for waxing. So it wasn't hard to find people who performed the procedure; they were listed by the hundreds in the Yellow Pages. I thought, okay, just pick one, should be no problem. Right? Wrong.

Because of the planned surgery, the pubic hair in, on, and around my labia had to be permanently removed. It was far more than a simple bikini wax. But because that's what most technicians were familiar with, I had to begin my phone interview of a potential electrolysis practitioner a bit different.

"Hello. Do you do electrolysis on the bikini line?"

The typical response was, "Yes, we sure do."

I went on. "Can you do it on the stomach hairline as well?"

"Yes."

At this point, I would take a deep breath and enunciate very carefully so they would understand me the first time.

"Okay, um...how about the labia area, for surgical procedures, things like that?"

"Oh, no. We do work on those kinds of people. We'll do males for that type of thing, but we aren't comfortable doing females. Sorry."

Click.

At that point pretty much all of them would just hang up. I was astounded. I thought, what the hell?! You'll do a Brazilian wax on somebody but won't do medical electrolysis. So, you'll wax an ass, but not zap an ass?

That didn't make sense, and I was becoming frustrated in my search to find a qualified technician. For a brief moment I considered learning to do ass zapping as a side job.

I finally went to the San Diego LGBT Community Center for help, and they directed me to one technician who worked on transgender persons. She was located in El Cajon. I gave her a call and was delighted to discover a wonderful person who was also very interesting. Not only was she herself a male-to-female transgender, but she was also a lesbian. She was willing to do my electrolysis, and that's all that mattered to me.

She charged fifty dollars per session, and I was looking at about three hundred hours of electrolysis in order for the hair to be completely removed. Another expense.

It was obvious I had to look for a second job that would allow me to work around my fire department schedule. This was going to be difficult. I began to have a whole new appreciation for people who train for the Olympics. Like those folks, I was on a mission and wasn't about to stop now.

My old high school friend Alice managed a pet store in Encinitas, just north of San Diego. I decided to ask her if she was hiring. I had worked for her before, so she knew I was a good, reliable worker. I only needed part-time work, and when I needed time off for surgery, she would understand.

The thought of trying to explain all this to any other potential employer was frightening. I couldn't come up with a lie to explain what really was taking place, nor did I want to. I'd have enough of being uncomfortable with myself. I was finally on a path to change all that, and working for Alice was the only choice that made sense.

I called her and we made plans for me to come visit her at home. I wanted to first tell Alice about my decision to undergo a gender change, which would then pave the way for me to ask for a job. She really wasn't surprised, of course. Actually, I hadn't shocked anyone so far.

After I told Alice, she said that if it made me happy, that was all that mattered to her. She told me I could work part-time every other day for eight hours, no problem. I could start right away.

I was getting more excited as I realized I was well on my way to affording the expenses associated with the surgery. The extra income enabled me to start hormone therapy as well. I also scheduled the bilateral mastectomy, and sent my deposit to Dr. Biber for my consultation. The only thing that remained was to inform the people I worked with at the fire station.

I wasn't sure how I was going to go about this just yet. I needed to do it tactfully to ensure I didn't lose my job. Despite all the harassment I had put up with, I really loved my job and it provided a good living. Additionally, I needed that money to carry out my plan for reassignment and all the other expenses I would incur on the road to finally become a male.

I decided that my first step would be to research discrimination laws. I wrote to my congressman, Ron Packard, and received a letter from his office indicating they had scheduled me for an interview with one of his assistants. She and I met for several hours and she provided information on transgender rights, discrimination, issues and harassment in the workplace. She said that if I had any issues, be sure to let her know and they would be more than happy to assist me with the matter. I felt good about our meeting and went on my way.

I decided to talk with my chief during my next shift, and tell him my plan. He was a good chief, and we often sat outside together to smoke. He would share stories from his childhood and growing up, how he had run away from home at thirteen to join the Merchant Marines.

He reminded me of my childhood teacher, Mr. Rodarte. They were very different in appearance, though. A heavy smoker, the chief was very thin and appeared older than his late sixties. He had short white hair, a mustache, and always wore a v-neck T-shirt and lots of gold jewelry. And he drove an old tan VW Rabbit. Man, he cracked me up, though some-times I think he amused himself more than anyone. He had retired from a fire department up north before coming to this one. I felt confident I could tell him what was going on, and what would be taking place.

That night after dinner, the chief and I went to the picnic table out back to have a smoke. He opened the conversation.

"What's up, kid?"

Suddenly, I was scared. My heart was beating so hard, it felt like it was going to jump right out of my chest. My face felt hot and flushed, and I felt close to vomiting. I thought to myself, *my god, just get on with it. Just say it, for Christ's sake.* Easier thought than said.

It felt like everything was happening in slow motion. A scene from *A Christmas Story* played through my head, the one where Ralphie, who wants a BB gun for Christmas, is sitting on Santa's lap at a department store. Santa asks him, "Hey kid, what do ya want for Christmas?"

Ralphie had dreamed about having a BB gun for so long, that it seemed like some kind of fantasy to actually tell Santa what he knows his parents don't want him to have. Ralphie couldn't think straight, so he chokes and just says, "A football."

On his way down the slide he finally spills the beans about what he really wants, but Santa denies him, replying with the same words every other adult has told him. "But you'll shoot your eye out, kid."

As that scene flashed before my eyes, for a moment I wondered whether the same thing would happen to me. I'd been silent for more than a couple minutes, trying to figure it out. I guess the chief must have thought I'd gone what he called addlepated (dull-witted) for a moment.

He asked, "Is something wrong?"

I took a deep breath and went for it. "No, Chief. I guess I just needed to talk to you about something."

"Okay," he said, putting his hand out as though giving me a clear road to venture down. "Go ahead, then. What's on your mind?" He paused, then added, "Oh, wait. Do I need to light another cigarette for this?"

"Yeah. In fact, you might want to light the whole pack before I'm done," I answered. "Well, the thing is, I wasn't quite truthful when I told you I wasn't going to have a sex change."

Taking a drag of his cigarette, he said, "Okay," giving me permission to go on. Encouraged by this, I continued.

"I'm really going to do it. I'm sorry I lied to you but didn't have all the facts and information, and wasn't sure how people would react when I told them. I wanted to make sure I did everything appropriately; not just for myself, but for everyone I work with."

"Okay, I see," he responded. "Hmm, well now. I've known several lezzies in my day, dykes is what we called 'em, y'know. I've seen a lot in my career. I've been known to say that I've seen everything, and y'know, after knowing you, I can say I really have seen everything in my fire department career."

He was just shooting the shit with me, and being really straight. He wasn't freaked out or shaken up, just talking with me like always. This really meant a lot and helped me launch into the rest of the story.

"Chief, I spoke to my therapist. She and I want you to know I would like to extend an offer to make arrangements to have her and a doctor who specializes in transgender people in the workplace come speak to human resources and the personnel department. They'll also come speak to department heads as well as firefighters on any station. This way there is no confusion, rumors or misleading information."

I continued. "There'll also be counseling and stress management available to the firefighters who might feel the need for that. I will not ram this down anyone's throat. I'll continue to use the same bathroom. I'll promise to make this a slow and easy transition process, so not to disrupt the department and the focus of what we're here for. I know we're in the business of being firefighters and I love my job with all my heart."

I don't know if I'd ever made a speech that long before. I paused, waiting for his reaction.

In his normal tone of voice, he then simply said, "Okay. I appreciate how you've gone about it."

He smiled and said he would notify human resources on his next shift. He would also talk to the other station chiefs and captains before the firefighters were told. I was instructed not to say anything to anyone, and just wait until it was worked out with the higher ups, and Chief had spoken to me again.

He really wasn't surprised and asked if I thought I would be happy. I said yes, and then shared with him that I had been on the verge of suicide for many years, and it boiled down to a matter of life or death.

At the end of the conversation, he warned, "Just be ready. You might get some shit, y'know, but stand your ground and be prepared to take it. Don't tattle for every little thing those idiots might pull. Remember, you're the first to do this in the federal fire department, and when you're the first at anything, you have to pave the way for the rest. If you quit, then the ones who follow you will lose."

He got up from the bench. As he walked away, he turned back with a half-smile and added, "Good luck, kid. Don't let 'em fuck with you. I'll be watching." Then off to bed he went.

I was confident he would handle it, and the situation would be okay. Maybe not smooth, but okay.

Firefighters are ruthless, and show very little mercy if they don't like you. At times, they can be worse than women when it comes to gossip, storytelling, and other goings-on. Much worse. They talk just as bad about their wives and girl-friends as women do about their men. They look at nude photos, talk about having sex, who they did, what position they did it in, what toys they may or may not have used, how drunk they got, and what disease they caught along the way.

The entire time they're regaling you with what is always way too much information, they're usually scratching their nut sack and sticking their chest out like a bunch of proud roosters in a henhouse. So you can imagine how terrified I was to tell them, "Oh yeah, by the way, I'm going to have a sex change."

I usually got along with most of the guys. A few had even asked me out, knowing full well I was a lesbian. Of course I acted flattered, but in no way was I interested in what they had. On the other hand, I *was* interested in getting what they had for myself, and wasn't looking to window shop their models.

I figured most of the guys would be okay with what I was doing. To my mind, I was having a dick added, not a brain transplant. I would be the same person. Having a penis would not make me a different person, although it has been said men do think with their penis. Bearing that phrase in mind, I once kidded Dr. Biber, and asked him if brains came with the penis, or were they extra? He just laughed and said they hadn't come that far yet. Until they do, I would have to use the brain I was born with.

I continued to work at both the fire department and the pet store. After each twenty-four-hour shift at the station, I drove forty minutes up the road to the pet store to work eight hours more. I had one day each week to squeeze in therapy, endocrinology appointments, and electrolysis, not to mention laundry, grocery shopping and everything else I needed to do. I chose Monday as my personal day to take care of business.

A few shifts later, Chief called me into his office. He had spoken to human resources, who had a meeting and then got in touch with my therapist and doctors. They were going to tell all the firefighters in my battalion together to help prevent rumors and gossip.

Members of our personnel department would be there along with human resources, the battalion chiefs and station captains. They asked that I not be present so firefighters felt free to ask questions they might not ask if I were there. Human resources also suggested that firefighters be allowed to speak to someone individually if they had issues. They were also encouraged to speak to me in confidence to ask questions about anything they didn't understand. I would arrange to be there along with my therapist to answer any questions.

Come that first meeting, none of the firefighters knew what was happening. They just saw a bunch of people from human resources come into the station along with a bunch of white shirts, also known as fire chiefs. Firetrucks from other battalions rolled up, and then people they'd never seen before arrived, namely my therapist and some doctors. Everyone was wondering what the hell was going on. I was the only firefighter who knew what was about to take place.

"All firefighters muster in the training room," the station speaker announced. I felt like I was going to be sick but reminded myself that soon it would all be over with. That's how naïve I was. In reality, the battle was only just beginning.

I would loved to have been a fly on the wall or dust bunny in a corner that day, so I could have heard what was being said. I only heard little bits and pieces of what took place. I'll never know what really happened.

For the next four hours I paced around the station's bay floor, wondering what was going to happen and what they might say after. When the door finally opened, I heard talking mixed with laughter, and wasn't sure what to think. When they came out, no one said anything to me, they all just acted normal at first, like the calm before the storm.

I was called into the chief's office for the Reader's Digest condensed version of what was said. Apparently, there were mixed emotions and questions, which were understandable. This was new to everyone, including me.

The biggest concern was the bathroom, and some were afraid I would want to see their penis. I let the chief know he could assure the boys I didn't want to see their penises before, and I surely don't want to see them now.

I said, "Besides, mine will be brand new. Why would I want to look at theirs? I'll have my own to admire."

Comebacks had become my defense mechanism. I think they were really afraid of their own curiosity. I could relate. If I had been in their position, I might be curious, too.

Some of the firefighters wondered if I was going to like men now. This floored me. I said to the chief, "Their intellect just amazes me. I hope that the therapist gave some insight on that? Because what I'm changing is my gender, not sexual preference. But I can see where their confusion comes in."

I really couldn't, though. I wondered, can these guys really be that stupid? Chief and I shared a few laughs and then he warned me it was going to be a bumpy ride, but to hang in there. He gave me the names of the few he thought I might have a problem with, even though he wasn't supposed to. He assured me that for the most part, they were told they would have to deal with it or find another job. He and I both knew that wouldn't keep them from harassing me when others weren't around.

At this point, my inner happiness overshadowed the bold cruelty I experienced at the station. I didn't understand what had really changed. I was the same person they had liked, joked with, ate dinner and watched TV with. Some had even hung out with me on days off.

Would a firefighter funeral been better to attend than a meeting about someone getting a penis and finding happiness?

Hey, fellas, y'know, I opted for living instead of suicide. Sorry that upsets your little apple cart. But I want a penis so my body can match my mind. Sorry you hate me for it.

That was how I felt.

Suddenly, the guys who hadn't paid any attention wanted to have sex with me because they thought it was kinky, kind of a she-male thing. Two guys who kept asking me on dates were angry. One transferred to a station out our battalion and never spoke to me again. The other continued to have feelings for me and made himself miserable, crazy, or probably both.

Several of the guys who liked me at first now disliked me; others said they didn't agree with my decision, but I was the same person. Some just said, "Whatever. It's not my issue."

It was a mixed bag of reactions, and I didn't get it.

In 2016, 1,497 female-to-male
surgeries were performed in the U.S.

AMERICAN SOCIETY OF PLASTIC SURGEONS (2016)

CHAPTER ELEVEN

Family circus

Informing my coworkers was now done, or at least had started. Now I had to begin telling friends and family. On one hand I didn't care what they thought, yet on the other hand I did. Because of the nature of my relationship with my mother and sisters, I figured what's the worst that could happen? They decide not to speak to me? That wouldn't have been a surprise.

I had reached a point where I felt like I just couldn't be hurt anymore. I gave up begging family to love or like me. My mother had alienated most family members from us, leaving just her, my two sisters and me, so there wasn't much family anymore. The best-made family is comprised of those whom you choose to have in your life anyway, and those often are not your blood relations, at least not all of them.

I decided to just suck it up and get it over. I called my mother and said, "Hey, Mother, what's up?"

She gave her usual witty reply, "The sky. What's up with you?"

I pushed onward. "Oh, nothing, I just wanted…"

She cut me off. "You getting sick?"

"No, why?"

"You sound like it, that's why."

Looking back on this conversation, I give her some credit for at least noticing something different. The hormones had begun to change my voice.

"Well, what if I told you I wanted to have a sex change? What would you think? Would you care?"

She replied, "Why would I care why you do what you do?" She paused for a second, and then said, "Now you'll *really* look like your dad—a real butthole!" She burst into gales of laughter.

I just listened and when she finished, I said, "Okay. Well, I am going to, have one that is. It's in Colorado, and I am going to do it. Just thought I'd tell you."

Her next response virtually ended the conversation. "If you have the money to do that, then you have the money to pay me back what you owe me."

It would be a while before my mother and I spoke again.

Next, I called my older sister Kari. She said, "Whatever. I could care less. I always wanted a brother, anyway."

So she accepted it right off with no problem. I then called my younger sister Sara, who was living in Tennessee, with her dad after he divorced Mother.

When I told her, her response was more complicated. On the one hand she questioned my decision. "Why? God made you the way he did, and why would you change that?"

She then made a quick attempt at being supportive but canceled it out. "If you do, I'll love you as my brother, of course. But I don't agree with what you're doing. It's against God."

I knew she meant well. Unfortunately, she passed away from a tragic accident in 2004. At least I know she loved me for who I was.

As for my friends, well, they became few and far between. I had many lesbian friends until I wanted gender reassignment surgery. Suddenly I had almost none. At one point, I wasn't even allowed to enter the old bar I used to work at without a female escort. I was told, "You have to have an escort. This is a lesbian bar."

I was also told, "You should figure out you're a lesbian, just accept it and stop trying to change it."

How could I be shunned by the very community I'd been part of for years? In the end, I lost a lot of friends. Only a handful have stood by me, and I'm thankful for their loyalty.

I worked two jobs to save up enough money to undergo the bilateral mastectomy but instead of traveling to Colorado, I elected to have it done by a local plastic surgeon in Escondido. As long as I had a letter from both my therapist and Dr. Biber saying I was transitioning, the local surgeon was willing to perform the mastectomy. I should expect to be off work for eight weeks. No driving allowed.

By this time, my menses had all but stopped. I never really had much of a period anyway. I planned to change the gender on my driver's license following the mastectomy.

The day came when I had enough money to schedule the mastectomy. I arrived at Dr. Smith's office in Escondido. He said, "Are you ready?"

I nodded my head and said, "Yes."

They prepared me for surgery, the nurse inserted the IV, and the doctor drew incision marks on my chest using a purple pen. When I woke up, I was never, ever going to wear a bra again. Thank god! I slowly counted backwards, ten. . . .nine. . . . and then faded out.

"TJ, how are you feeling? You are in the recovery room. You did very well and are almost ready to go home," said the nurse.

I was driven home by a friend and went to bed. I had very little discomfort at the surgical site and needed pain medication for only a couple days. I was able to walk and stretch, and felt so happy. It was almost as if the joy suppressed the pain.

I was supposed to be on bedrest for eight weeks, so the surgeon was shocked when I recovered in four and a half.

Although strange at first, I felt like a new person. One day I had breasts, the next day I didn't. Never again would I hear someone say, "Do you need some help, sir?" while shopping for bras, or look at me like I'm a store pervert.

When I saw my flat chest for the first time, I laid on my bed and cried. I could finally look at myself and almost see me. Try to imagine Ken's head walking around on Barbie's body. Most people would stare, right? That's what I felt they were doing to me. For the first time in my life, I could go out into the world and not feel ostracized. Now, I finally felt more like Ken. People identify you by face, facial hair, basically from the breasts up. They don't know what's in your pants.

While healing, a neighbor across the way tried her best to date me. I wasn't in any shape to be dating, nor in the mood. I told her I was a pre-op transgender person, but that failed to deter her. In fact, it made it worse. She was almost like a stalker after that, even asked me to marry her.

I ended up moving in with a good friend. Having a roommate to share expenses allowed me to save more money each month. Before we moved in together, she was kind enough to bring over food and help care for me. I figured if I lived as her roommate, it would make it easier for her to care for me during the next surgery.

The day came when I could finally return to full duty. The only person left in my family to notify was my birth father. I hadn't made contact with him in some time, so I decided to call him. He answered the phone and I said, "Dad?"

"Yes," he replied.

"This is TJ. How are you?"

"Hey, haven't heard from you in a while. How ya doin'? Still workin' for that fire department you were workin' for? How's come ya haven't called in a while? What's new?"

I didn't expect that many questions from him and wondered what other ones he might come up with once I told him.

"Yeah, I'm still there. So... I wanted to tell you something."

"Okay, then. Whatcha wanna tell me?"

I hesitated for a moment. "Well, I haven't called in a while because I was afraid you wouldn't talk to me, not after I told you I was going to change my sex."

"Hmmmmm," he responded. "Well, okay. You were liking girls all along, and that's okay by me. So, I still …well, that's okay, TJ. You do what you gotta do, and just keep calling, that's the main thing. It's okay with me. Alright?"

"Okay, Dad. Thank you! And I love you. I will call you."

"Okay. Bye, then. Here is Beverly."

He never told me he loved me; he would just put his wife on the phone. However, I completely believe my biological father loved me and accepted my change in his own way. He just couldn't say it in so many words.

TJ before his transition (1991).

It's a helluva start, being able to
recognize what makes you happy.
LUCILLE BALL

CHAPTER TWELVE

Business as usual

My first day back at the fire station after the mastectomy was rather strange. I showed up like I would for any other shift except now I had no breasts. Pretty much all the guys were quiet. A few said, "What's up?" Others didn't say anything.

It was uncomfortable at first, of course. They also had to remember to call me *he* instead of *she* now. It was going to be quite a change for everyone.

I suppose no one really knew what to say or do. I understood that this was a unique situation for everyone involved. I had some empathy for them, unsure how I would react myself if I had been in their shoes. I chose to handle the situation with as much care as possible. I tried not to ram it down anyone's throat and took extra care to be aware of their feelings as well as my own. I was the one who was disrupting the norm, so I did my best to smooth things over.

But the favor wasn't returned. I heard their snickers when they called me a he-she, she-male, or simply It, which made me feel like the hairy cousin on *The A••ams Family.*

They did what they called *The Crying Game* walk. When I was sitting in the TV room, one of the guys would walk past me with his penis tucked between his legs while singing *The Crying Game* song. Some just flat out refused to call me *he* and always said *she*. In those cases, I just didn't answer.

Once when I was sitting alone at the picnic table smoking a cigarette, an older black man who had always spoken to me walked over. He put one leg up on the bench and lit himself a cigarette.

"What's up, Bob?" I asked him.

"Nothin'," he replied as he rubbed his hands together, followed by a long drag on his smoke. He nodded his head, so I knew he was going to say something more. He looked around to make sure no one else was listening, then bent over and said in a quiet sort of way, "Why you doin' this, man? That's some freaky shit, you know? Your kind really don't belong here in the firehouse, y'know? You ain't gonna last long here, you know dat, right? So why don't you do yourself and your brother firefighters a favor and just quit?"

He gave me a little wink as if he'd just put me wise. Taking another drag from his cigarette, he spun around smugly as if his mission was accomplished and started to walk away. My childhood rage began to well up inside. Oh, hell, no! *Hell*, no! He did *not* just say some shit like that to me!

It felt as though everything happened in slow motion. I got up from the bench and said words I never thought possible. They came rushing out like a river.

"Bob! Fuck you, nigger! Who the fuck you think you are, telling me I don't belong here? You ignorant black asshole, try this on for size—you don't belong here, either, you know that? Trying to fit in as a firefighter…shit! I mean, being a firefighter is a white man's job, right? You don't belong here no more than me. So why don't you take your black ass on back to the back of the bus where you belong, you dumb nigger!"

I stomped away. I was so angry. Of all people, he should realize what it feels like to be a minority. Later that night, I saw him walking toward me and I thought, *oh, god, not again.* But he surprised me. "TJ, I thought about what you said, and you know, I'm sorry, man. I never thought about it that way."

"Bob," I replied, "You of all people should know what it feels like to be faced with prejudice. At one time this job didn't allow black men to work as firefighters. Now along comes me—I'm a different minority. As a matter of fact, a minority times two."

I continued. "I'm a female in a male profession struggling to prove I'm an equal, and now I'm a female trying to become a male. It's really no different than having to ride in the back of the bus until you jump through some crazy stupid hoops in order to earn the right to sit in the front, or in any seat you want. It's a dumb game set up by an unfair society, but that's what I'm doing here, trying to get to the front of the bus. I'm taking my turn in the back for the time being. Each day I struggle for acceptance, for the right to be happy, to live in peace so I can sit in the front. One day I will sit in the front of the bus, or in whatever seat I want to without judgment or persecution. Every race, gender and creed have to take their turn in the back of the bus."

I stopped and took a breath. I wasn't accustomed to giving speeches, although this particular speech is one I have repeated many times since in classroom lectures to help educate audiences about what it means to be a transgendered person.

Why does every genre of society who has come through such prejudicial treatment seem to think they're the only ones?

Everyone goes through it in some way or another, some for longer than others. You're forced to sit there until society deems you worthy of their acceptance, then you can move to the front. Then it's the next person's turn to sit in the back and wait for acceptance.

Why is it that we humans treat each other this way? I do not understand it. Yet after we had that chat, Bob and I became closer and had a better understanding of one another.

I continued to receive harassment in the department from several firefighters all the way up to captains and fire chiefs. More than once I was told, "Why don't you just go ahead and leave? It would be for your own good."

Others went so far as to say, "You better watch your back, you never know what can happen."

Or, "Your kind isn't wanted here."

Some even just looked me in the eye with a steely gaze and asked, "What would it take to get you to leave?"

I didn't know if they were planning to offer me a bribe or beat me within an inch of my life. I kept going and tried to ignore their behavior. Some of the guys asked questions like, "Can we see your chest now?" Or wanted to know if they could see my surgery when I was done.

Word of something this unusual always travels like wildfire, so it was only a matter of time until I became a subject of interest to people around the region, including the media. I was contacted by a local news station as well as the National Enquirer.

I decided to do a three-part news story because it offered insight as to why I was doing what I was doing. Not only that, it allowed the firefighters to actually have the opportunity to speak up and give their perspective as well. There were few who spoke on my behalf.

I did not do an interview with the National Enquirer because as a gossip magazine, I feared they would turn my story into something it wasn't. I did speak at colleges around the area and was invited to be a guest on two talk shows, Jenny Jones and Gabriel Carteris. I appeared on the Gabriel Carteris show with my therapist and my first wife. I was unable to make the Jenny Jones show due to a snowstorm. I also appeared on a show called Strange Universe.

I really wasn't ashamed of what I was doing or who I was. For the first time in life I felt happy and normal. Just one thing bothered me, though, and to this day I've yet to figure it out. Why did my happiness make other people miserable?

I continued to work both jobs and save money, not allowing myself to spend an extra dime unless I had to. I didn't go anywhere or do anything. My focus was work and surgery. I had a goal and was going to meet it.

While working at the pet store, I became good friends with one of my coworkers, Kelly. I wasn't prepared to get involved with someone, of course, but things do happen. She and I became involved in a short matter of time, although I wasn't yet finished with surgery. And no, she was not a lesbian.

I guess in a way, Kelly gave me the attention I needed at the time, and in a sense I suppose I settled. I swore I was going to sow my wild oats when I had my chance, and go out with every woman I could, but I didn't. I ended up thinking I might not be able to be with anyone else, so I'd better grab her while the grabbing was good.

One thing led to another and we moved in together. I did care for Kelly but knew I should have thought things through a bit more. Born a Taurus, the practical nature of this zodiac sign always wants to trust that things will work out. I didn't see all the red flags. Or rather, I chose to ignore them.

Kelly and I married in spite of it all, kind of like desperate marries delirious. After so many of her extramarital affairs, I finally filed for divorce.

At that time, I still was pressing on and taking it from the guys at the fire station. One captain harassed me nonstop. He said his religious beliefs kept him from accepting what I was doing. He could not deal with the fact that I was now allowed to use the men's bathroom, or what I had decided to do with my body. Why were people so concerned with the fact that I wanted a penis? They acted almost like they were jealous, or maybe they were envious, I wasn't sure. It was becoming a regular topic of conversation. Guys would ask, "How big are you going to get it?"

"You should lay that bitch out like a speed bump."

"Are you going to name it?"

Some numnuts asked, "Do you get it from a corpse?"

Still another, "What if you get a black one?"

I was asked if they could see it, if I was going to have big balls, the list went on. I just told them, "Who wants big saggy balls? I will have a nice firm nut sack, how about that? And if you want to see my *crank*, as you call it, you can pay a non-refundable hundred dollars to reserve a viewing right now. Come on, cough it up, don't miss out! And there'll be another hundred dollars due at the showing."

Some took me seriously and tried to offer me money. And they thought I was the freak.

CHAPTER THIRTEEN

A whole new me

I had saved up enough money to undergo the first surgery in Colorado. Scheduled for February 17, 1995, this surgery would construct my penis and testicles. I called my mother and asked if she wanted to go, to be with me—and there for me.

"No, there is no reason for me to go, you have someone. Why should two of us go?" she replied.

I tried to explain that I needed her there for support, that it was important to me to have her part of my life. She said she didn't like my girlfriend Kelly, and if my girlfriend was going, she would not. I would have to choose between them.

I wasn't going to do that. I couldn't handle that kind of stress on top of worries about the surgery itself. I was very hurt and upset that my mother would even say such a thing. But then, given her track record, I shouldn't have been surprised.

It was our first trip to Colorado, and Kelly and I went by train, a twenty-four-hour ride. The night before, I shaved my head knowing I was not going to be able to bathe for a week.

We arrived in Trinidad, Colorado, considered to be the sex-change capital of the world. A small town of just over eight thousand, it was lined with brick buildings and streets. I felt like a bug under a microscope, as though everyone knew why I was there.

The hotel picked us up from the train station. We checked in and went to our room. The place looked like the Bates Motel—old and decorated in blues and pinks.

The next day I met with Dr. Biber, a veteran war surgeon who had moved to Colorado from Korea, because the small town needed a surgeon. One day in 1969, a social worker asked Dr. Biber to perform a sex change on her, and his new specialty was born.

His office was three flights up inside the historic National Bank building. We climbed the stairs to his office. I checked in at the front desk, and recognized Marie's voice from our phone conversations. Marie had the oldest filing system I'd ever seen, and the office lacked many modern conveniences.

All kinds of people were here. Marie smiled and asked me to take a seat in the large waiting room which bore an old red cross on the tile floor. Was it representative of the Red Cross or some kind of religious statement? As odd as it was, I decided it likely was not intentional, and had just been there since the building was constructed.

I was relieved to have gotten this far with my mission. I'd stuck to my master plan and here I was, at last. But I would be lying if I said it all felt like it was going to be a piece of cake.

I met with Dr. Biber the day prior to surgery. He wanted to examine me, discuss the procedure, and talk it through— once surgery is performed, there was no changing back. We spoke for quite some time about my job, relationship, and my plans for the future. Dr. Biber was quite impressed that I was going to remain at my job as a firefighter. Apparently, a lot of people go elsewhere after transitioning. As I left his office, I realized that by tomorrow, half my transition will be complete.

The next morning, I entered Mt. San Rafael Hospital. As I started filling out paperwork and paid the fee, the lady at the front desk gave me a really strange look. "Come on in. Male to female, right? Here is the paperwork you will need to fill out, living will, medical directive and other general information," she said. And then added, "For precaution only."

I looked at her and said, "No. Female to male."

She smiled with surprise. "Oh, you're a female? I'm sorry. I thought you were a male already, going to be a female. You are so handsome. I was thinking what a shame you wanted to be a female. We aren't supposed to think or say that, though," she added, as though she had said too much.

I breathed a sigh of relief and said, "Oh no, that's okay. No problem."

I completed the paperwork and was then escorted down the hall and checked into my room. I was instructed to put on a gown and wait for the nurse.

First things first was an enema. The nurse laid me on my side, inserted the enema into my rectum, emptied the contents of the bottle and instructed me to lay in that position, holding the fluid for two minutes before releasing it in the toilet. I was then wheeled down the hall for an IV. It was beginning to feel like an assembly line.

As the anesthesiologist asked for all my pertinent information, for a fleeting moment I had second thoughts. What will my life be like? How will people treat me? Why didn't my mother come with me? Thank god I will feel normal at last.

I then heard Dr. Biber say, "You ready, kid?"

"Yeah, I sure am."

He winked as he put his hand on my shoulder. "I'll see you in there then. Before you know it, you'll be the new you, okay?"

He smiled as he walked away. Just like Mr. Rodarte from junior high days.

The surgery Dr. Biber was scheduled to perform was a hollow tube abdominal pedicle graft. Basically, the procedure surgically constructs a penis using tissue graphs of skin, nerves and veins harvested from my abdomen just above the pubic area. Dr. Biber would then implant new silicone testicles.

Once inside the operating room, I laid there thinking, here goes. I then thought, TJ, you do some crazy shit, but you are finally gonna be happy. On that thought, I drifted off under the anesthesia's influence. I don't remember anything else until I woke up.

While under general anesthesia, Dr. Biber made an 8 cm incision and removed a flap of skin to make both the urethra and the shaft of the penis. The larger tube is basically rolled up around the inside tube, using more skin taken from my thigh in an area devoid of hair.

Once that was finished, Dr. Biber constructed my new set of testicles. He had to do dissection of the labia on both sides, then put a silicone implant in each. This was stitched up, and apparently I withstood the procedure very well.

I woke up as a dude.

A few hours later I heard a nurse say, "You did really well! How are you doing? The doctor would like you to drink something to get your bowels moving, okay?"

I thought, my god, I went in for a new penis, not a new set of ears. She was talking so loudly, I got up right away and started walking around just to get her to be quiet. Dr. Biber came by and said he had never seen a patient get out of bed directly after surgery and walk the halls so fast.

With each surgery I endured, it was as though an emotional weight was lifted from the deepest part of my inner soul. The pain and recovery were nothing compared to the years of mental torment, emotional torture, taunting, teasing, and being ridiculed my entire life.

At long last, I felt as though I was slowly setting myself free and becoming the person I should have been born as. At the same time, I was able to slowly start forgiving those who did or said cruel things to me over the years.

As I lay recovering in Mt. San Rafael Hospital, each day getting better, Kelly was outside roaming the halls, smoking, or on the phone. She wasn't by my side, yet I didn't mind. I was smiling inside, without a care in the world.

On the third night in the hospital, my temperature spiked and my left inner groin was hot and painful. Dr. Biber came to see me, and walked in wearing a cowboy hat, jeans, boots, and a jacket vest. He asked how I was feeling.

"Not so well," I answered.

He looked over his handiwork as he examined me. "Well, you got your money's worth, didn't you? I hope y'know I hand-picked those balls just for you, straight from one of my own bulls out at the ranch."

In addition to performing sex change surgeries, Dr. Biber was also a cattle rancher. He continued, "With a set like that, you can do anything."

As he looked down at the inflamed area, he said, "Hmmm, yeah, you have a small hematoma, no problem."

Snapping his fingers, he said, "Nurse, give me a local and a fifteen-inch scalpel."

Then returning his commentary to me, he added, "Don't worry, kid. I'll have this fixed up in no time. You'll be alright."

He gave me a local anesthetic, sliced open my groin and drained a pocket of blood.

"See the blood coming out? Just let it heal," and with that, he left.

I eventually healed enough to go home. I was required to stay for seven days or longer but my primary doctor at home had agreed to take out the stitches, so I was allowed to leave the hospital a bit sooner. Kelly and I boarded the train and prepared for the long ride back to California.

I did well upon returning home but then my abdomen started to feel swollen and I again developed a fever. I didn't know what to do so just laid on my side and held my stomach as my temperature continued to climb.

Suddenly, I felt a small amount of moisture in the palm of my hand. I sat up, and then stood up. As I did, a pinhole stream of foul-smelling bloody pus came out of my abdomen. I went into the bathroom, stood in the bathtub, and dialed Dr. Biber. As I waited to be put through to him, the stream grew bigger. I finally reached Dr. Biber and told him what was happening.

"Just relax, kiddo. It's a hematoma. Just squeeze it until nothing else comes out, then go to the E.R.," he calmly said.

I did exactly as he had instructed. It was the most bizarre thing I had ever seen, and left a large hole which finally closed on its own.

I returned to work wearing larger pants while the surgical site healed, which would take about two months. At that time Dr. Biber would then release the graft, complete the surgery, and I'd be done. It was kind of like having a suitcase handle detached. When I worked my second job, I wore overalls. At home, I wore sweats.

With paperwork from Dr. Biber stating I was transitioning, I was finally able to get the gender legally changed on my driver's license. I went to the Department of Motor Vehicles, walked up to the counter, handed the lady my license and said, "I would like to fix the sex on my license, get it changed from female to male."

Before I could finish my sentence and hand her the paperwork, she took my driver's license and said, "Oh my, I am so sorry they have you in the system as a female, Mr. Barganski. Let me fix that. There's no charge for that; you should have a new license in the mail within a few weeks. Is there anything else we can do for you?"

"No, thank you," I smiled and left.

The same thing happened at the Social Security Office. I didn't have to show any paperwork. I used to have to argue with people who didn't believe I was a girl. Now they were falling all over themselves with apologies for putting the wrong gender on my documentation. All I could do was laugh.

At the fire station, it was a little awkward at first. I was glad I wore big pants. People tried hard not to look, yet were so curious. What a strange trip, coming to work having your crank (as they called it) be the talk of the department. They all wondered about the size, how long, how does it work, what does it look like.

Eventually, a few of them started to ask me questions in roundabout ways. Others were angry and hated me for it. I was told several times, "Why don't you do all your brother fire-fighters a favor and just make a new life someplace else? Start over where no one knows your story. If you had a real dick in the first place," they added as they grabbed their crotch up and down, "you wouldn't have needed to get one of your own."

It didn't stop there. "Why don't you come over and watch a real man fuck a chick so you'll know how to bang really good?"

And I thought I was the freak.

Our annual physicals were performed by a military doctor at a nearby base. The civilian doctor who had seen me every year understood my situation, but he had retired and been replaced by a Navy physician who didn't know my history.

Every year, most males must undergo a prostate exam. When I entered for my turn, this new doctor obviously hadn't read my chart before seeing me because the first thing out of his mouth was, "Drop you pants."

"Did you read my medical record?" I asked.

"No," he said. "Is there a problem?"

"Not really," I replied. "It's just that I don't need a prostate exam because I don't have a prostate."

"Oh," he muttered as he looked through my record. He suddenly got wide-eyed and cleared his throat. "Well, I guess I can just check you're . . .whatever you got, then."

"What?" I shouted. "No! I will be right back."

I got up and went straight to the front receptionist, whom I knew. I recapped what the doctor said. Her eyebrows went up, she excused herself to go talk with the doctor. She returned to get me and I returned to the exam room. The doctor apologized, asked me a few general questions and I was done.

I went back to the fire station and told my chief, and we had a good laugh. Chief said, "You probably made the poor guy submit his retirement papers!"

I thought to myself that instead of being an ass about it, I'll just have to prepare some comebacks for ignorant people. From then on, I started joking about it, and in the end had the last laugh.

The harassment at work continued and I was moved to a different station. Because of the situation, I was sent to a smaller station that was known as the "station of diversity."

No one liked that station because it hardly received any calls. The firefighters didn't like the captain, and the four that were there were sort of department misfits. The captain was a goofy sort of guy, as in Gomer Pyle goofy. Always smacking his mouth and shaking his head. When we went to the gym, he wore black knee-high socks, red shorts, a pink muscle shirt and blue tennis shoes. Colorful. He wore his pants high and his fire cap low. An interesting study in appearance, yet he was one hell of a nice guy.

The engineer was a black guy who was recovering from substance abuse. His days were up and down, and I never knew how he was going to be from day to day. We had our moments together, both good and bad. Yet, if it weren't for some of the talks we had, I don't know how I would have gotten through some of the rougher times in my life. Not just with my change, but all the adjustments I went through later on. He talked a lot of bullshit yet was a good friend who set you straight and took no shit off anyone else.

There was the little white guy who dressed and acted very feminine. At first he was nice to me but turned out to be a two-faced arrogant asshole. Finally, there was the Hispanic guy who quoted scripture all the time and stayed up at night to pray and watch religious channels. Even though he struggled to love himself, he never judged others.

This had to be the strangest group of guys I had ever met. Throw me into the mix, and it truly was a diversified station.

One day we were outside standing by the firetruck when the chief, the deputy chief, and assistant chief came by. The chief had a big smile on his face and kept swaying back and forth, clapping one fist into the other hand. "So fellas, how y'all doing today at station sixteen? Wow, this sure is a diversified station now, isn't it?" he smirked.

We looked at each other. The black guy said, "Now ain't that some fucked up shit to say. What's that supposed to mean, diversified?"

Chief said, "Well, you know."

"No, we don't know. Why don't you tell us?"

"Ha, ha," the chief laughed a bit nervously. "Okay, well, you guys look like you're busy, so see you next time," and they all left.

We made fun of them after they left, yet it opened a scar of old emotions that were trying to heal. It felt as though when you try to move forward, it seems as though someone wants to push you back and not allow you to let go of your misery.

I was intensely focused on my goal and pressed on, working both jobs and saving money. My relationship with Kelly seemed okay at the time; it was familiar and oftentimes fun. Without thinking clearly about what was in my best interest, we were soon engaged. I guess I figured it wasn't going to get any better than that. Maybe this would be my only opportunity to have a family and be normal. Maybe no one else would accept me as a transgender person. Kelly was the first person who acknowledged me for who I was. We decided to marry after I had healed from the final surgery.

Two months passed and I was ready for the final surgery. I called to schedule it, and the only available date was May 3, 1995. I couldn't believe it. It was going to be complete on my twenty-ninth birthday. What were the chances of that?

Kelly and I drove this time, with her friend coming along on the ride. We stayed at the same hotel in Trinidad as last time. They were good to us, and cheap to boot. The hospital was just down the street.

I met with Dr. Biber the day before, just as I had the prior two times. I found out that his birthday was on May 2, we were both a Taurus. We discussed how things were going, and the final stages of the procedure. He advised me of the complications that could arise, and I was on my way.

The following morning I checked into the hospital. I already knew the routine involved with the administrative end of things, and it hadn't changed. The last surgery was finally at hand. I entered the operating room to complete the transformation. I had waited so long for this day to come, and now here I was being reborn on my birthday.

Dr. Biber released the abdominal pedicle graft and then formed the glans, the head of the penis, and grafted it onto the shaft that had been surgically preformed two months prior. He then proceeded with a panhysterectomy, surgical removal of the uterus, ovaries, cervix, and related lymph nodes along with a partial vaginectomy. This final surgery was not complicated because the majority of it had been performed during the first surgery.

I was taken to my room for recovery. When I woke, I was anxious to see the results but it was all bandaged up. Naturally, when I was able to see it, it had many sutures in it yet there it was—my very own penis.

It was red, swollen, and full of sutures. I called it Frankenweenie for a while, and hoped it didn't look like that for long. Dr. Biber said it would get smaller as the swelling went down.

All in all, it was about six inches long. Dr. Biber said I drove too far to get cheated. The man was an amazing surgeon, a kind human being, and had a great sense of humor.

Once again I didn't have to stay as long as expected because my primary doctor in San Diego was willing to remove the sutures. Within a few days, I was ready to return home to San Diego. Dr. Biber wished me well, hugged me and said goodbye. I realized I would actually miss him.

He told me to keep in touch, and I did for quite some time. His birthday is the day before mine. He called me a couple times to have me talk to patients, which I didn't mind at all. We kept in contact until he died in 2006, after contracting pneumonia during a cattle drive. He saved my life and he was a great loss to the transgender community. No one else does the intricate, realistic procedure in the female-to-male surgery the way he did. He was truly a wonderful person.

CHAPTER FOURTEEN

I am, I said

So, here I am. The whole me. This is what I wanted.

Am I happy? Yes.

Do I feel like I belong in the world? Absolutely.

For the first time in life I could finally go out without feeling like people were staring and pointing.

I finally felt free.

I had a new life ahead of me, even though I had a lot to adjust to. There would be some negative things along with the positive, but I knew I would adapt.

It took a while to adjust to my new physical self. At first, the penis felt heavy and I felt more modest. At work, it seemed as though everyone was looking at my crotch. Some asked what my penis looked like, others asked to actually see it. Still others asked whether I had gotten it from a donor.

No. I didn't. It came from my own skin.

I wore underwear beneath my swim shorts to hide what people might think was an erection. It was also hard at first to take my shirt off in front of certain friends and family members, such as my mother. My older sister had always accepted me, and her children already called me uncle. Although they knew about the surgery and don't care, it goes back to an insecure body image and my hypersensitivity over those who wanted to see my new penis.

I was also worried people would ask about the scars on my chest from the mastectomy. Of course, they've faded and are now minimal, and I have hair on my chest so no longer have those same modesties. My wife teasingly says it looks like I'm smuggling produce in my jeans. As time went on, I became more comfortable in my new skin.

And then there's the matter of sexual intimacy. Everyone wants details. How does it work? The answer depends largely on whom you are with. The first time I used my penis, I considered myself a virgin. While my penis works, and I do have erections and orgasms, it doesn't produce sperm. Otherwise it's a fully functioning penis and set of testicles.

I married Kelly shortly after the first surgery. We tried to have children by artificial insemination through the fertility center. I was matched with a donor who looked very much like me, but our attempts failed. Sadly, Kelly was unfaithful during our marriage and in some ways I was glad not to have had children with her. We divorced after five years, parting as friends and going our separate ways.

I wouldn't change anything for the world, not even the experience I went through. That's what has made me the person I am today.

Some feel sorry for me as a poor unfortunate guy who was born female. Born into the wrong body, dealt a bad hand, had a rough life, walked a hard road, who finally underwent sex reassignment surgery to find happiness. It's true that most of my childhood sucked. Had I been born a boy, my life would have been very different, I am sure.

Maybe if my parents had been better at parenting, I would have been a different person. But truth be told, I'm a better person for all I've been through and who I've become.

I believe we are here for reasons, and perhaps my reason for being here is to help others such as those who are born like me and believe there is no hope for them.

We hear many stories of males transitioning to female, but not female to male. Because of the mindless chatter, jokes, comments, and other ridiculous prejudices, I'm hypersensitive about being one of the few courageous ones who transitioned from female to male.

Today, believe it or not, I work in the medical field for a doctor who, when a transgender patient came into the clinic, said, "You're fucking kidding me! Can you give that patient to another doctor?"

I said, "Okay," but just had to ask, "How come?"

"Oh," he replied, shaking his head, "In medical school we were made to tolerate those kinds of patients, not to treat them. They have so many mental problems. You can see those freaks a mile away, and I just don't like dealing with that shit or those kind, y'know what I mean? They are fuckin' weird."

He wore glasses. I told him he might need his prescription checked.

"Huh?" he blinked.

"Oh, never mind, I was just wondering how far a mile must look to you."

I roomed the patient who had transitioned from female to male, who was there for an upper respiratory infection.

I want to rewind a bit to my final years at the fire station. From 1992 until 2005, I was the recipient of verbal harassment and abuse. A few of them were openminded and I considered them friends, but they'll remain nameless for their own safety. I would hate to have them tarnished because they were willing to accept me.

I never could figure out why my own happiness made others so miserable. How did my decision to transition my gender affect others? If a person chooses to do something in their personal life that makes them happy, and it doesn't hurt anyone else, how can that happiness cause others to behave with resentment and hate? Is it because we dared to pursue happiness? That's a question only they can answer, I simply have to accept that I'll never know. In the long run, I guess it really doesn't matter. I'm so relieved to finally be happy with who I am.

One fire chief once said to me, "If I had to go through half the things you have in your life thus far, I would have probably killed myself already. But you just keep going, and with a smile on your face. How do you do that?"

I took a moment and then said, "Chief, sometimes I don't know. It's day by day. I do know this—I feel sorry for all those who don't know me, whose minds are led by ignorance; those who judge me because I choose to have a penis. No matter what, we can always find fault in someone to justify disliking them. That's human nature."

I then added, "Mirror, mirror, what do you see? What you like and don't like about me is only what you do and don't like about yourself. Envy is a bitch, ain't it?"

He stood there for a bit and then said, "Yeah, I guess so. Tell you what, TJ, one thing's for damned sure. You have more balls than most people I've ever met," he chuckled.

As for other coworkers, I tried to accommodate their feelings because I know my decision was an adjustment for everyone. But it came to a point where enough was enough. I didn't get special privileges or treatment like some thought. I had to buck up like everyone else. Most of the guys refused to call me *he* even as years passed. They refused to share space with me willingly. Live and let live.

My thought process goes something like this. If you or someone you loved were in a life-threatening situation and needed help, and I was the only person who could save your life or that of your loved one, would it matter whether I had a penis or a vagina? I guarantee that my gender doesn't matter when giving lifesaving chest compressions or dialing 911.

One chief did stick up for me, but she couldn't always be there. She was a good friend, and remains so to this day. Many of the guys wanted me to quit or get fired. I brought my children and family to the station just like everyone else did. I could not allow them to intimidate me. I continue to keep in contact with those who supported me.

Life went on and in 1999, I remarried a woman named Lisa. Some friends cautioned me against it. "TJ, don't do it."

I figured there was just something about Lisa they didn't like, so I ignored their advice and did it anyway. In looking back, I see I was eager to pursue my dream of happiness. My only regret was that Lisa asked me not to tell her parents about the sex change. I figured, who cared? It was in my past. I had already changed my birth certificate, driver's license, and social security card. What would be the big deal?

We had a big Catholic wedding and later had a beautiful baby boy via artificial insemination.

A year and a half later, Lisa took my entire 401(k), fought in court to overturn my birth certificate in an attempt to sever my parental rights, claiming she had no idea I was transgender. To top it off, she sued me for child support and forced me in bankruptcy. Caught smack dab in the middle of this whole fiasco was my son, Dillin.

An estimated 1.4 million transgender people in the U.S.
don't have affordable access to gender transition surgeries.

AMERICAN SOCIETY OF PLASTIC SURGEONS (2016)

CHAPTER FIFTEEN

I should have seen the light

I first met Lisa online. It was the age of computer dating and meeting people from around the world. I was home recovering from ankle surgery, and decided to explore online dating for myself.

At the time, I was a thirty-three-year-old firefighter with my own home. Lisa sent me a message from the dating site, and I replied. At the time, photos were not required and we could go only by what someone said in his or her profile.

We eventually exchanged photos and soon started chatting on the computer every day, which then turned into talking on the phone. Lisa lived near San Francisco, and we continued talking on the phone for several months. I learned about who I thought Lisa was, and she learned about me. We planned to meet face-to-face for the first time.

Lisa wanted to come down to San Diego instead of me traveling up to her place. I assured both Lisa and her mother that Lisa could stay with my friend, Vicky. She was coming only for the weekend, so Vicky said she would hang with us as sort of a chaperone and, if Lisa felt uncomfortable at any time, Vicky would drive her back to the airport. Having Vicky join us proved to be a blessing when Lisa and I filed for divorce.

The first night, the three of us went to dinner in old town San Diego, and then for drinks at a local bar. I knew I had to tell Lisa about the sex change at some point. Although I don't feel obligated to tell everyone, I do feel it is important to tell those I'm intimate with, or those friends who I love and trust.

I made sure Vicky was present when I told Lisa. For a moment I felt sickly, and then just let the words tumble out. "Hey, just wanted to let you know that in 1995, I had a gender change from female to male."

Lisa just looked at me for a second and replied, "Okay. Everyone has skeletons in their closest. As long as my parents don't find out, I don't care."

It was a red flag for me, yet we had a good weekend. Lisa and Vicky stayed the entire weekend at my place.

Our dating was short lived, and Lisa soon moved down to San Diego. I then discovered that while in San Francisco, Lisa had been living and sleeping with a married man who already had four kids and didn't want more. Lisa was trying to have a child with him when he decided to reconcile with his wife. Their relationship ended.

During my divorce from Lisa, he and I had several conversations. Lisa's motivations and deceitfulness came clear to me after we married in December 1999. Her parents paid for an enormous Catholic wedding with over two hundred people in attendance. We spent our honeymoon in Hawaii.

Upon returning to San Diego, we bought a home together and began planning to have a baby. We went to a local sperm bank and after searching through several profiles, the doctor said, "I have a donor that could be your twin."

He handed us the profile and after looking it over, we purchased three vials of semen. We began to track Lisa's cycles. When she was ovulating, I picked up semen from the clinic and inseminate Lisa. It worked, and our son Dillin was born in February 2001.

At the time, I had no idea what Lisa was planning. Now, it tears my heart out. What she did is something I wouldn't wish on any parent.

Dillin was three months old. Lisa's mother had come down for the weekend. I left for my shift at the fire station and when I returned home the next day, Lisa's car was gone and my house was empty.

TJ with Dillin (2002).

The neighbor said that Lisa and her mother brought in a U-Haul truck. Her friends came over and they managed to clean out the entire house in less than twenty-four hours.

Everything was gone, including Dillin.

CHAPTER SIXTEEN

She took it all

With Lisa and Dillin gone, what was I going to do? Why did she do this? She said that she just didn't want to be married any longer. I eventually learned that this was her plan all along. Both Dillin and I were caught in Lisa's web of lies, deception, and manipulation.

Lisa hired a lawyer and served me with divorce papers. She claimed she had no idea about my gender reassignment surgery. She said I had deceived her, and requested an annulment of our marriage based on the fact that it wasn't legal to marry a woman.

Lisa and her attorney asked the same judge who granted my birth certificate gender change to reverse it back to female.

If the judge granted her this, she could have my name removed from Dillin's birth certificate. It backfired. The judge fined Lisa $1,500 plus attorney fees for harassment on the fact that she had prior knowledge of my birth certificate change.

Initially the court granted me 75% custody of Dillin. Since I had majority of the custody, Lisa was forced to move back to San Diego. But she continued to fight for more. When things didn't go her way, we went back to court.

The parenting plan was eventually changed to 50/50 but Lisa still wasn't happy. When Dillin was five, she petitioned the court to grant her a move-away order. It felt like someone nailed a spike in my heart. When the day came to hear the judge's ruling on her request, my attorney recommended I not be present. I had one more day to spend with Dillin before Lisa took him away.

Dillin suffered emotionally throughout this time yet Lisa continued to attempt to alienate him from me. By the time he was fourteen, she finally succeeded. He's now nineteen, and I still feel an indescribable pain of not knowing when I'll see my son again, if ever.

Despite the darkness, my future held one glimpse of hope. I had reunited with Misty, my old friend from the Navy. She was now divorced with two children of her own. I went to see her a few times and our friendship turned romantic. Misty was living in Florida, and when Lisa moved away with Dillin, I decided to start fresh.

I retired from the fire department, packed up what I had, and drove to Florida. My old company commander lived near Misty, and I enjoyed being able to see her again.

The court had granted me a five-week visit with Dillin, and ordered Lisa to fly with Dillin to Florida. I was excited yet nervous. Would Dillin even know who I was?

When he saw me, he reached for me, rubbed my face, and said, "Daddy."

I held him tightly, and whispered, "I love you," in his ear. In that moment, time stood still.

Dillin is now a nineteen-year-old handsome young man. Misty and I have been married for eight years now, and we live in Washington State. Retired from the fire department, I continue to work in the medical field and live just like everyone else. Although I wish things had turned out differently with Dillin, I have no regrets. He will always be my son, and I his father.

Christmas 2015

CHAPTER SEVENTEEN

Branches

This last and final chapter describes and tells why I wrote this story. I didn't do it to make a name for myself, or to embarrass or humiliate any family or friends. I wrote this book for my own peace of mind. It was quite therapeutic and gave me a sense of release from all the emotional things I had been carrying inside throughout life, things that had caused me to feel hate for others as well as myself, where no hate belonged.

The writing made me take a deep look at who I really was, as well as who other people were, where they came from and what they were about. I realized this wasn't just about me, but about everyone and everything. About how we as individuals don't even realize how we truly see each other or feel about each other until it slaps us dead in the face.

When we look at our own prejudices, we often discover that we're truly all the same. We have been to the same places and fought the same fight in one way or another. No matter who we are, we have all taken our turn, each and every one of us, in the back of the bus.

Somewhere in our life we have struggled with something that no one agreed with. We fought to make them believe that what we want or want to do is best, so we move from seat to seat making our way until we finally get that front seat. May my story inspire you to fight your way forward just as I have.

CHAPTER EIGHTEEN

Q&A

What body differences did you notice when you started hormone therapy?

At first, I didn't notice any body differences, the transition was slow. I've always had somewhat of a masculine physique. I guess it was no different than going through puberty all over again. I let the hair on my legs and underarms grow. I never really had acne during puberty, so I didn't have much of that during the transition. My voice has always been fairly deep. My sister actually has a deeper voice than me and she never took hormones.

Slowly I started to notice some hair on my chest, not much. I then noticed facial hair slowly coming in. I kept my face clean shaven for a long time while I worked at the fire department. I couldn't have a beard or goatee. Having facial hair was new to me so I didn't really care if I had facial hair or not. I never really defined myself by being able to grow facial hair. Also, at the time beards were not really in style.

Looking back, I just didn't have a lot of body changes from taking hormones. I always had a very light, irregular menstrual cycle and when I started testosterone, they stopped altogether.

Which testosterone dose did you take, and do you still require hormone treatment?

I took testosterone cypionate 1,000mg/10mL injections. For several years, I went to the endocrinologist every two weeks for an injection into my upper arm, thigh, or buttock. About five years after the final surgery, I felt no benefit from the hormones and stopped. I continue to grow facial hair, my voice remains the same, and I don't seem to have any feminine qualities.

What's the biggest takeaway you noticed once you started hormone treatment?

My biggest takeaway from hormones is weight. However, my weight has always fluctuated so even the weight changes from hormones weren't major changes for me.

What kind of medical follow-up does the hormone treatment require?

Of course, with any medication you have follow-ups. I had my hormone levels checked regularly to make sure they weren't too high or too low. My doctor has said that if I ever want to start hormones again to let him know. It's never off the table for me. I can always go back on testosterone if I want.

What physical adjustments did you face upon returning home from surgery?

I didn't have many physical adjustments after surgery. I still sit down to urinate. The only difference is that I use the male bathroom. Of course, I had already been using the male bathroom for a while. When my surgery was done, Dr. Biber had not yet perfected how to reroute the urethra, so mine is still in its original place. That surgery is available to me, but I can't see spending another $15,000 just to stand at a urinal.

What emotional adjustments did you face upon returning home?

I had to learn to be a man at work. I stayed in the same job where I was already being ridiculed by most of the department, and now it was worse. My skin became thicker. I heard the taunting, the teasing, snickering and laughter by the guys.

"Wonder what it looks like."

"Where did he get it from?"

"Probably came from a dead guy."

I just let it go, what else could I do? I loved my job and told myself I could endure the twenty-four-hour shift at the fire department but would drive home in tears. I dreaded going to work every day. My heart would pound in my chest and it felt as though I would have a heart attack. I internalized my anger, put a smile on my face and just did my job. My friends were my comfort. They were my family. I surrounded myself with those who loved and accepted me. That emotional support made all the difference.

What spiritual adjustments did you face?

I did not have any spiritual adjustments. I was not and had not attended the Mormon church in quite some time. Most of my family and friends accepted me so there was no real spiritual adjustment.

Did you experience any postsurgical complications aside from the two hematomas?

With the exception of two hematomas that resolved with time, I did not have any medical complications.

How did you handle post-reassignment intimacy?

It's important for individuals to be honest with potential partners. I never deceived an intimate partner. If I made the choice to be intimate with someone, they were aware of my status and where I was in the process. I do not think it is fair to deceive anyone. Be upfront. There is someone out there for everyone. Slow down, and love will find you.

Did you continue counseling/therapy?

I continued counseling for a short period of time because I stayed working at the fire department and it was so stressful. I couldn't burden my friends with all I was going through at work. It was important to me to get a better understanding of how to deal with what was going on. It was an adjustment for everyone and I had to take that into account. I'm not saying what they did or how they treated me was right, no way. They didn't know how to deal with what was happening. I didn't either. This was in the middle of don't-ask-don't-tell time.

What are the biggest adjustments for transgender people after surgery?

It's different for everyone, but looking in the mirror and finally seeing a body that matches your mind and believing it is really you is an adjustment. There's a fair amount of pinching yourself to make sure you aren't dreaming.

Do you feel counseling/therapy is helpful for those considering sex reassignment surgery?

Yes, I can't stress this enough to anyone who is considering sex reassignment surgery. This is a lifelong change and a commitment to living your authentic self. This is serious and not something you treat like a trend or new fad. Once you have surgery, you can't reverse it. I highly recommend a minimum of one year of therapy with a qualified clinician who is experienced in gender dysphoria.

You had a number of therapists who offered different diagnoses yet never suggested sex reassignment. What advice would you give therapists who have a patient like you?

I think therapists should not be too quick to suggest sex reassignment surgery. Take time with the patient to build a therapeutic alliance. Support the patient in processing gender identity first. Once the patient is secure in that identity then approach the idea of surgery. I can't emphasize enough that this is not, and should not be, a quick process. This is major surgery. No surgical procedures should be taken lightly. Counselors should spend time focusing on honesty.

What advice do you have for parents who are raising a child with gender dysphoria?

My advice to parents raising a gender dysphoric child is to exercise unconditional love, understanding, and patience.

Allow your child space to process their identity, and support them whatever the outcome. It is not your job to like or dislike their gender identity. It is your job to love, accept, and support.

Does it benefit the transgender person to know they have clearance from a mental health professional, or is it really to make others feel more comfortable with your decision? How do you feel about clinicians who serve as gatekeepers to body modification?

Having clearance is important. A good clinician can help the individual process the decision. A good clinician can also clarify the diagnosis. Is it really gender dysphoria, trauma, or something else? Again, this is a life-changing process and not something to be taken lightly. I don't look at the therapist as the gatekeeper. I look at the therapist as someone who can first determine the diagnosis and then support the transition. It takes honesty on the part of the individual to build a strong therapeutic alliance.

If it's important to clarify the transgender's motives for body modification, what do you want counselors to know?

It's important for the individual to be honest about his or her history. The counselor/therapist should be open to exploring trauma, overt and attachment-related traumas, to help clarify the diagnosis.

What do you want readers who walk the same journey to know? Should they proceed with sex reassignment? What should they look out for when searching for a surgeon?

I think it is important to understand that this is not a quick process. This is a journey—not something that happens overnight. Embrace the process, which means being open and honest in counseling.

Take your time and research surgery. Don't expect your insurance provider to cover everything. Do not expect faith-based hospitals or clinics to support you. Accept that their point of view is not yours and move on. One question to ask yourself—are you doing this for yourself, or are you trying to change the minds of the religious right?

Research and understand the different surgical options and accept that travel might be required. Look at this as an investment in you. Also, buyer beware. If your surgeon offers discounts, strongly consider looking elsewhere.

Ask questions. What is the aftercare like? If travel is required, where am I going to stay? What does the procedure entail? If your surgeon is not willing to walk you through the process and ensure you understand the surgery, then you might what to keep looking.

How has society's perception changed about transgenders in the past 25 years?

I think people are definitely more open about being transgender, yet people are more confused. It used to be about being male or female. Now it's about being gender fluid, gay/straight and so on. I think this really confuses people, and generally speaking, people are less afraid when they're less confused.

For whatever reason, there will always be some who don't accept you. Forget those people and just be yourself. I never introduce myself as a transgender person. I am TJ. I transitioned a long time ago. I am not a trans-guy. I am just a guy.

How has the medical community's perception changed?

I have a friend who is a doctor. From our conversations, I've learned that most doctors get very little information or introduction to transgender unless they specialize in the field.

While working at an urgent care, one doctor said to me, "TJ, stop putting those transgender or sexual people in my rooms. They just have mental problems; I can see those people coming a mile away. They just want hormones."

Interesting that he can see transgender people coming a mile away but couldn't spot me standing right in front of him and working alongside him for three years.

If you could go back and do this all over again, what would you do different?

Nothing. I am happy with who I am. I feel like I have lived and am living an authentic life. I share my status when there is value in doing it. I have never tried to hide who I am or deceive someone.

What did you learn most about yourself during this journey?

I learned that despite all the things that have happened to me, I am a strong, determined person. I have learned firsthand that society treats men and women differently. For example, I have had contractors come to my home to do work. They always talk to me regardless how many times I tell them, please talk to my wife. They will talk down to her like she has no idea what they are talking about. When they talk to me, they use a lot of technical terms or assume that I know what they are talking about.

What is the final takeaway you want readers to know about your story?

Just be true to whomever you are. Don't segregate yourself from society. You are more than what bathroom you use. Don't be defined by your genitals. At birth, none of us are guaranteed happiness. Happiness comes from living a meaningful life.

Acknowledgments

I want to thank my awesome wife Misty for helping me with my memoir, especially the typing, reading drafts, giving advice and seeing this book through. To my two boys, Dillin and Phil, thank you for loving me and letting me be your dad. I love you both very much.

Thank you to my family who continue to love and respect me. Thank you to my counselor Theresa Waters who has been an emotional rock for eleven years. Thank you to all my childhood friends who continue to be part of my life, and my lifelong friends who have been part of my life before my change and remain my friend to this day. You have continued to show me love regardless. I love you all so much. Thank you to the AlyBlue Media team for all of your hard work and patience in getting this book published. Special thanks to Lynda Cheldelin Fell for believing in me and my story.

About the author

Terry J. Barganski was born biologically female on May 3, 1966, in
southern California. After graduating
from high school, he worked for the
U.S. Forest Service and the California
Department of Forestry fighting fires
for six years. He joined the U.S. Navy
in 1989, and served two years on the
USS Emory S. Land during the Persian Gulf war. After leaving
the Navy, TJ returned to fire service in southern California,
and later became a firefighter/EMT.

In May 1995, on his twenty-ninth birthday, TJ under-went the final surgery that would complete his transition from female to male, and finally begin living life as a man.

After being diagnosed with degenerative disc disease, TJ retired as a firefighter/EMT in November 2005.

Because of a general lack of awareness regarding female-to-male gender reassignment, TJ now speaks to behavioral science students who hope to become therapists. He helps them to better understand the issues that individuals like him face, and also raise public awareness.

In addition to sharing his story with academia, TJ has appeared on news channels, talk shows, and was a guest expert on the television show Strange Universe.

TJ continues to work in the medical field, and write in his spare time, sharing his story and life experiences.

EMAIL: tjbarganski@gmail.com
WEB: alybluemedia.com/Barganski

ALYBLUE MEDIA TITLES

PARTIAL LIST

Letters to Matt

Survivors

Faces of Resilience

Barely Breathing

Who Took Molly Bish?

Color My Soul Whole

Remembering My Child

My Grief Diary

Grammy Visits From Heaven

Grandpa Visits From Heaven

Daddy Visits From Heaven

Faith, Grief & Pass the Chocolate Pudding

Crimson Sunshine

Heaven Talks to Children

A Child is Missing: A True Story

A Child is Missing: Searching for Justice

Grief Reiki

Hidden Truths Within

Where have all the children gone?

GRIEF DIARIES

Surviving Loss by Overdose

Surviving Sudden Loss

Through the Eyes of a Widow

Surviving Loss by Cancer

Surviving Loss of a Spouse

Surviving Loss of a Child

Surviving Loss of a Sibling

Surviving Loss of a Parent

Surviving Loss of an Infant

Surviving Loss of a Loved One

Surviving Loss by Suicide

Surviving Loss of Health

How to Help the Newly Bereaved

Surviving Loss by Impaired Driving

Surviving Loss by Homicide

Surviving Loss of a Pregnancy

Hello from Heaven

Grieving for the Living

Project Cold Case

Poetry & Prose and More

Through the Eyes of Men

Will We Survive?

Victim Impact Statement

Surviving Loss of a Pet

REAL LIFE DIARIES

Living with a Brain Injury

Through the Eyes of DID

Through the Eyes of an Eating Disorder

Living with Endometriosis

Living with Mental Illness

Living with Rheumatic Disease

Living with Gastroparesis

Through the Eyes of a Funeral Director

INTERNATIONAL GRIEF INSTITUTE

Aftercare Solutions Manual

iCare Grief Support Group Facilitator Manual

iCare Grief Support Participant Workbook

iCare Church Support Facilitator Manual

iCare Church Support Participant Workbook

iCare Grief Ministry Guide

iCare Grief Ministry Workbook

iCare Chapter Leader Manual

iCare Chapter Workbook

Humanity's legacy of stories and storytelling
is the most precious we have.

DORIS LESSING

*

She, He, & Finding Me

PUBLISHED BY ALYBLUE MEDIA
Inside every human is a story worth sharing.
www.AlyBlueMedia.com

Made in the USA
Las Vegas, NV
15 November 2022

59559302R00109